SUBSTANCE ABUSE ASSESSMENT, INTERVENTIONS AND TREATMENT

SUBSTANCE ABUSE AMONG ADOLESCENTS AND ADULTS

SUBSTANCE ABUSE ASSESSMENT, INTERVENTIONS AND TREATMENT

Additional books in this series can be found on Nova's website under the Series tab.

Additional E-books in this series can be found on Nova's website under the E-books tab.

SUBSTANCE ABUSE ASSESSMENT, INTERVENTIONS AND TREATMENT

SUBSTANCE ABUSE AMONG ADOLESCENTS AND ADULTS

ISABELLE M. GIORDANO
EDITOR

Nova Science Publishers, Inc.
New York

For permission to use material from this book please contact us:
Telephone 631-231-7269; Fax 631-231-8175
Web Site: http://www.novapublishers.com

NOTICE TO THE READER

The Publisher has taken reasonable care in the preparation of this book, but makes no expressed or implied warranty of any kind and assumes no responsibility for any errors or omissions. No liability is assumed for incidental or consequential damages in connection with or arising out of information contained in this book. The Publisher shall not be liable for any special, consequential, or exemplary damages resulting, in whole or in part, from the readers' use of, or reliance upon, this material. Any parts of this book based on government reports are so indicated and copyright is claimed for those parts to the extent applicable to compilations of such works.

Independent verification should be sought for any data, advice or recommendations contained in this book. In addition, no responsibility is assumed by the publisher for any injury and/or damage to persons or property arising from any methods, products, instructions, ideas or otherwise contained in this publication.

This publication is designed to provide accurate and authoritative information with regard to the subject matter covered herein. It is sold with the clear understanding that the Publisher is not engaged in rendering legal or any other professional services. If legal or any other expert assistance is required, the services of a competent person should be sought. FROM A DECLARATION OF PARTICIPANTS JOINTLY ADOPTED BY A COMMITTEE OF THE AMERICAN BAR ASSOCIATION AND A COMMITTEE OF PUBLISHERS.

Additional color graphics may be available in the e-book version of this book.

LIBRARY OF CONGRESS CATALOGING-IN-PUBLICATION DATA

Substance abuse among adolescents and adults / editor, Isabelle M. Giordano.
p. cm. -- (Substance abuse assessment, interventions and treatment)
  Includes bibliographical references and index.
  ISBN 978-1-61122-933-2 (hardcover : alk. paper)
  1. Teenagers--Drug use. 2. Drug abuse. 3. Drug abuse--Prevention. I. Giordano, Isabelle M.
  HV5824.Y68S873 2011
  363.290835--dc22
2010047095

Published by Nova Science Publishers, Inc. † New York

CONTENTS

PREFACE

This book examines certain cases where social and psychological issues are present among adolescents and adults with substance abuse problems. Topics discussed include cross-cultural parent-child relations; prevention strategies for parents on adolescent smoking; the national youth anti-drug media campaign; cocaine-dependent patients with antisocial personality disorder and cognitive performance in chronic street drug users.

Chapter 1 - More than 6 million adolescents who have become addicted to tobacco will die of tobacco-related illness as adults. As tobacco use remains the leading preventable cause of morbidity and mortality in the United States, developing even more vigorous prevention programs is an important public health priority. Each day about 4,000 youths, age 12-17, will try a cigarette for the first time and about half will become daily smokers. From a socioecological standpoint, there are individual as well as contextual factors related to adolescent smoking. However, there are two important factors that deserve particular attention for their strong influence: peer and parental influence. While there is debate as to whether parents or peers have more influence on smoking (especially in late adolescence), parenting behaviors can affect affiliation with smoking peers. Previous research has identified several parental characteristics associated with adolescent's smoking such as perceived parental influence, smoking status, smoking-related prompting, parental monitoring, and expectations not to smoke. Parents who smoke are encouraged to quit while their children are young; nevertheless, children of smoking parents have lower rates of smoking when parents communicate strong anti-smoking messages and establish household smoking ban rules.

Information and guidelines available to parents about smoking prevention typically emphasize the importance of teaching children how to say no or walk away from cigarette offers, ensuring child involvement with sports or other extracurricular activities, talking with children about tobacco in the media, establishing household rules, and being aware of with whom and where children spend their time outside of the home. Healthy Generations, a study examining parental influences and adolescent smoking, found that parents are aware of some smoking prevention strategies (e.g., talking to children about smoking and involving them in extracurricular activities), but not all (e.g., knowing who their friends are). The research has also shown that what parents do know about prevention does not always translate into the actions they actually take against adolescent smoking. Despite the majority of parents in our study reporting that they discouraged their children from smoking by talking to them about its harmful effects on the body, less than 10% of the parents mentioned teaching their children to say no, knowing who their friends are, talking about family experiences, and keeping them occupied with sports. The majority of parents in the study were willing to participate in smoking intervention programs; however the biggest barrier in being able to do activities with their children was lack of time due to work. Future research on factors that can help facilitate implementation of smoking prevention strategies by parents is important for developing parent-related program components to reduce incidence and prevalence of adolescent smoking.

Chapter 2 - Adolescence is an important development time when there is a significant restructuring in youth's social networks and support systems. A number of studies emphasize the negative role that peer groups play in determining youth's substance use, while still other studies find that youth substance use can be mediated by parental attitudes, family connectedness and monitoring. The main goal of the present study is to explore some of these associations in two different cultural settings. Data were collected among middle and high school students (ages 11-20 years) in Southern Hungary (N = 1240) and students (ages 10-19) living in a mid-sized urban area in Central Alabama, U.S. (N = 1525). The self-administered questionnaires were identical in both places and contained items that asked youth about their substance use (smoking, drinking, illicit drug use), and the parental/family influences in their life such as parental monitoring and parental attitudes towards substance use. Using multiple regression analyses in both samples, results suggest that parental monitoring (e.g., when parents know where their children are) is an important protective factor regardless of culture. Likewise, being beaten by a parent is an important universal risk factor. However, some differences may also be detected, e.g., parental attitudes towards substance use is an important influence only among Hungarian youth, while family structure is a significant predictor of substance use among US adolescents.

Chapter 3 – The authors conducted a first open-label acute phase and long-term (5-year) follow-up study of fluoxetine in 13 adolescents with comorbid major depression and an alcohol use disorder, twelve of whom also had a lifetime history of having used cannabis. Cannabis-related symptoms were assessed using the DSM-IV diagnostic criteria for cannabis dependence. During the acute phase study, the number of DSM-IV diagnostic criteria for cannabis dependence significantly decreased among the ten subjects who exhibited any of those cannabis dependence symptoms at baseline. In addition, the number of subjects who met full DSM-IV diagnostic criteria (at least three criteria items) for cannabis dependence decreased from five to zero, which was a significant decrease. The medication was very well tolerated during the treatment trial. No subjects demonstrated current cannabis dependence at the 5-year follow-up evaluation. Based on the promising findings of this pilot study, the authors of this study were recently funded by the National Institute on Drug Abuse (NIDA) to conduct a double-blind, placebo-controlled trial of fluoxetine in adolescent patients with major depression and a comorbid cannabis use disorder (R01 DA019142). However, the results of that double-blind placebo-controlled study will not be known for five years.

Chapter 4 - Authorization of the National Youth Anti-Drug Media Campaign, a multi-media federal program to persuade America's youth not to use drugs, expired at the end of FY2002. H.R. 2829 (passed by the House on March 13, 2006) and S. 2560 (reported by the Senate Judiciary Committee on May 25, 2006) would reauthorize the media campaign, along with the other programs run by the Office of National Drug Control Policy (ONDCP). H.R. 5576, the House-passed appropriations bill that funds ONDCP, proposes $100 million for the campaign for FY2007. The media campaign's effectiveness has been questioned, and the program has engendered its share of controversy. Nevertheless, ONDCP, the office of the "drug czar," is optimistic that recent changes in campaign strategy will help to reduce illegal drug use by young people. This report will be updated as legislative activity occurs.

Chapter 5 - This study compared the efficacy of two commonly used treatment approaches (cognitive–behavioral treatment and contingency management) for the treatment of cocaine dependence among methadone-maintained patients with and without antisocial personality disorder (ASPD). This disorder is strongly associated with substance abuse and recent study findings provide a strong argument against the perception that substance abusers with ASPD are unresponsive to drug treatment.

Method: Patients were randomly assigned to four study conditions including cognitive–behavioral treatment (CBT), contingency management (CM), CBT with CM, or methadone maintenance (also the control condition). The Structural Clinical Interview for Mental Disorders–IV was administered to 108 patients to assess ASPD.

Hypotheses: The authors hypothesized that ASPD patients in the three treatment conditions (CBT, CM, CBT + CM) would have better treatment responsivity over the 16-week course of treatment than would ASPD patients in the control condition (MM). Moreover, we hypothesized that there would be a cumulative treatment effect among ASPD patients over the course of treatment, with good performance in the CBT condition, better performance in the CM condition, and optimum performance in the CBT + CM condition. Conversely, the authors hypothesized that the positive treatment effect of CM would decline for the ASPD patients once the incentive was removed (i.e., during the post-treatment outcome period).

Results: A two-way analysis of variance showed that patients with ASPD were more likely to abstain from cocaine use during treatment than patients without ASPD. The strong treatment effect for ASPD patients was primarily due to the CM condition. A series of regression analyses showed that ASPD remained significantly related to CM treatment responsivity while controlling for other related factors.

Conclusion: Monetary incentives appear to reduce cocaine use among substance abusers with ASPD more than among those without ASPD. The results of the present study and other recent publications suggest that substance abusers with ASPD may be more responsive to treatment than previously believed.

Chapter 6 - Clinical literature has long contained reports of cognitive decrements among substance abusing/dependent patients. However, the direct effects of chronic street drug use have been understudied to date. The paucity of research in this arena may be due in part to the myriad of co-occurring factors observed in treatment-seeking abusers of illicit substances. Factors such as alcohol dependence, psychiatric co-morbidity and medical disorders may confound the scientific investigation of cognitive decrements. In addition, more sensitive assessment strategies may also be needed to detect and characterize the subtle cognitive decrements associated with chronic drug use. The current chapter outlines these issues and presents strategies for addressing these concerns in the clinical research setting. A controlled laboratory study, designed to disentangle the cognitive effects of chronic street drug use in substance abusing subgroups, is also presented. The results of this study identify decrements of cognitive efficiency during a sustained attention task in detoxified, abstinent participants with a history of abuse of/dependence upon street drugs. Findings are discussed in the context of current trends in street drug research and the potential application of laboratory findings to the recovery of street drug users.

Chapter 7 - Background: Studies on neuropsychological functioning in alcoholism have reported cognitive changes, which have been interpreted in light of the frontal lobe hypothesis and the hypothesis of global brain dysfunction. Findings concerning the influence of family history of alcoholism on cognitive functions are inconsistent. Since cognitive functions may be relevant for the therapy of alcoholism, investigations of alcoholics in early abstinence are of critical importance.

Methods: Alcoholic patients (A) in early abstinence and healthy controls (C) were compared on a range of cognitive domains, including verbal and visual memory, prospective memory, memory for temporal order and executive functions (working memory, planning, verbal fluency). Analyses included a comparison of A and C. In addition, the cognitive profile of alcoholics with a positive (F+) and negative family history of alcoholism (F-) was compared.

Results: Group comparisons yielded verbal and visual memory deficits of alcoholics. Alcoholics were also impaired on alternate and phonemic verbal fluency. The two alcoholic subgroups with and without a positive family history did not differ significantly from each other on any cognitive measure.

Conclusions: The observed impairments in early abstinence are consistent with the hypothesis of diffuse brain dysfunction. Future studies using multidimensional designs are desirable to investigate the influence of family history on neuropsychological functions and the association between cognitive measures and relapse in further detail.

Chapter 8 - The pursuit for happiness is, perhaps, the most common instinct and the most persistent driving force in humans. In fact, the great majority of our goals are directed to this end. However, in spite of all the progress that modern society has developed for entertainment, communications, ease of domestic tasks and improvement of countless ailments, our search for happiness is frequently unfulfilled. Two main evidences point out a huge gap between our everyday activities and our perception of human satisfaction; these are the large proportion of depression among the general population and the identically large proportion of addictions to both, legal and illegal substances. Although the issue of addiction to drugs is extremely complex, it is important to consider the very basic circumstance that the craving for any neurotropic recreational substance lies in cerebral substrates and responds to the most understandable of human wants; the feeling of pleasure. From cigarette smoking, to alcohol, to psychotropic medicines and illegal drugs there is a continuum; humans become devoted users just because their molecular effects on some areas of the brain. From a simplistic clinical perspective, it is easy to understand the reasons for failure of therapeutic actions in the fight against addictions; any addiction is easy to acquire and awfully difficult to eliminate; most humans are predisposed to them and they are usually a result of the personal search in response to either one of two ubiquitous feelings; sadness or desire for happiness.

Research on the neural mechanisms involved in addiction should be increased, particularly directed to prevention in those subjects prone to addiction due to genetic or constitutional susceptibility. Comprehensive multidisciplinary approaches must be implemented because most singular interventions currently used, either medical, social or judicial have been largely ineffective.

Versions of these chapters were also published in *Journal of Drug Addiction, Education and Eradication,* Volume 3, Numbers 1-4, and Volume 4, Numbers 3-4, edited by Frank Columbus, published by Nova Science Publishers, Inc. They were submitted for appropriate modifications in an effort to encourage wider dissemination of research.

In: Substance Abuse among Adolescents   ISBN: 978-1-61122-933-2
Editor: Isabelle M. Giordano   © 2011 Nova Science Publishers, Inc.

Chapter 1

PREVENTION STRATEGIES FOR PARENTS ON ADOLESCENT SMOKING: A GAP BETWEEN WHAT THEY KNOW AND WHAT THEY PRACTICE

Christina K. Holub[1], Jeanette I. Candelaria[2]
and Rafael Laniado-Laborín[3]
[1] University of North Carolina at Chapel Hill, USA
[2] San Diego State University/University of California, San Diego, USA
[3] Universidad Autónoma de Baja California, México

ABSTRACT

More than 6 million adolescents who have become addicted to tobacco will die of tobacco-related illness as adults. As tobacco use remains the leading preventable cause of morbidity and mortality in the United States, developing even more vigorous prevention programs is an important public health priority. Each day about 4,000 youths, age 12-17, will try a cigarette for the first time and about half will become daily smokers. From a socioecological standpoint, there are individual as well as contextual factors related to adolescent smoking. However, there are two important factors that deserve particular attention for their strong influence: peer and parental influence. While there is debate as to whether parents or peers have more influence on smoking (especially in late adolescence), parenting behaviors can affect affiliation with smoking peers. Previous research has identified several parental characteristics associated with adolescent's smoking such as perceived parental influence, smoking status, smoking-related prompting, parental monitoring, and expectations not to smoke. Parents who smoke are encouraged to quit while their children are young; nevertheless, children of smoking parents have lower rates of smoking when parents communicate strong anti-smoking messages and establish household smoking ban rules.

Information and guidelines available to parents about smoking prevention typically emphasize the importance of teaching children how to say no or walk away from cigarette offers, ensuring child involvement with sports or other extracurricular activities, talking with children about tobacco in the media, establishing household rules, and being aware of with whom and where children spend their time outside of the home. Healthy Generations, a study examining parental influences and adolescent smoking, found that parents are aware of some smoking prevention strategies (e.g., talking to children about smoking and involving them in extracurricular activities), but not all (e.g., knowing who their friends are). Our research has also shown that what parents do know about prevention does not always translate into the actions they actually take against adolescent smoking. Despite the majority of parents in our study reporting that they discouraged their children from smoking by talking to them about its harmful effects on the body, less than 10% of the parents mentioned teaching their children to say no, knowing who their friends are, talking about family experiences, and keeping them occupied with sports. The majority of parents in our study were willing to participate in smoking intervention programs; however the biggest barrier in being able to do activities with their children was lack of time due to work. Future research on factors that can help facilitate implementation of smoking prevention strategies by parents is important for developing parent-related program components to reduce incidence and prevalence of adolescent smoking.

INTRODUCTION

In this chapter, we will cover parental influences on adolescent smoking, highlighting the Health Generations study. This study aims to examine parent attitudes about adolescent smoking, parent knowledge regarding tobacco, and approaches that might be useful in developing prevention programs aimed at parents. But first, we will take a look at the epidemiology of adolescent smoking. To conclude, we consider how targeting parental influences on adolescent smoking can be integrated into more comprehensive multilevel prevention efforts. With this in mind, it is our hope to inspire further research leading to the development of promising prevention programs, ultimately increasing positive health outcomes for all adolescents.

Adolescent Smoking: A Public Health Priority

The leading *preventable* cause of disease and death in the United States is tobacco use. Its impact has not gone unnoticed with approximately 440,000 deaths each year, translating to an annual health-related economic loss of over 150 billion dollars [1]. Statistics such as these and both the short- and long-term consequences of tobacco use have been the impetus for the development of innovative, even more vigorous, intervention programs to reduce and prevent smoking [1].

Prevention efforts should begin with younger age groups, as many of today's adult smokers began when they were adolescents. Looking even further back, the factors that influence adolescents to smoke exert their effect beginning in childhood. While some programs have targeted high school students in their effort to intervene on smoking initiation, research shows that approximately one out of every six (17.4%) 9th grade students has already taken up the habit and approximately 1 of 2 (52.0%) has ever tried smoking (even one or two puffs) [2]. Eighteen percent of high school students report smoking a whole cigarette before the age of 13 [2].

Each day in the United States, approximately 4,000 youths age 12-17 try their first cigarette [3]. At this rate, it is estimated that 6.4 million children today can be expected to eventually die from a smoking-related disease such as cancer, heart disease, or lung disease [3]. Not only should we be concerned with future consequences, smoking in adolescence has also been linked to more depressive moods, low self-esteem, and low self-efficacy [4]. In addition, adolescents who smoke are more likely to experiment and use other illicit drugs such as marijuana and cocaine because of the various psychological, social, and pharmacologic factors associated with smoking [5]. As such, surveillance and the ability to track trends in adolescent smoking is crucial because it allows researchers and public health practitioners to learn more about the adolescents who are at risk for smoking initiation and can serve as a tool to evaluate intervention and prevention efforts (*see Research Highlight 1*).

Smoking in Secondary Schools

The Youth Risk Behavior Surveillance System (YRBSS) reports that almost 60% of high school students have ever tried smoking (even one or two puffs) [2]. Across state surveys, this percentage ranges from 32.8% (Utah) to 71.1% (Kentucky). The percentage of high school students who report smoking at least one cigarette in the past 30 days (current cigarette use) has declined in recent years, but the percentage remains high at 22%. Current cigarette use differs by race/ethnicity and by grade. White students have the highest rates of current cigarette use (25%), followed by Hispanics (18%) and black students (15%). The percentage of students who smoke increases with each year in high school with 17.4% of 9th graders, 21.8% of 10th graders, 23.6% of 11th graders, and 26.2% of 12th graders reporting current use [2]. Johnston and colleagues found that, even before entering high school, current cigarette use was reported by 9.3% of 8th graders [6].

Adolescent smoking has been declining steadily since its peak in the mid-1990's, but research shows this decline is near its end. Results from the Monitoring the Future (MTF) survey indicate that while the rate of decline has been slowing overall, in 2005 it actually halted for 8th grade students; and the end of these declining rates is also predicted to transpire into upper grade levels as well [6].

There are a number of factors that point to the end of the declining rate of adolescent smoking. Several indicators have leveled off from previous improvements including: seeing smoking as dangerous among both 8th and 10th graders, smoking disapproval among 8th graders, and perceived availability of cigarettes among 10th graders [6]. All of these factors point towards the need to continue addressing adolescent smoking as a public health priority and to developing new innovative prevention intervention programs.

PARENTAL INFLUENCE ON ADOLESCENT SMOKING

From a socioecological standpoint, adolescent smoking is associated with individual factors (e.g., demographics, self-esteem), social influences (e.g., family, peers), as well as contextual factors such as culture, media/advertising, and tobacco-related policy [4, 7, 8]. Taken together, there are many factors that influence an adolescent's decision to try a cigarette. Specific types of influence may affect adolescents differently or play a greater role in their decisions. However, there are two important factors that deserve particular attention for their strong influence: peer and parental influences.

RESEARCH HIGHLIGHT 1

The ability to monitor health-risk behavior trends among adolescents provides public health practitioners and researchers with feedback on what the most current issues are as well as information on the success of intervention efforts. These statistics not only inform the development of new programs, but can also serve to inform policy. These are two noteworthy, on-going studies that provide us with the ability to monitor the health of adolescents nationwide.

Youth Risk Behavior Surveillance System [2]

The Youth Risk Behavior Surveillance System (YRBSS) monitors six categories of priority health-risk behaviors among youth and young adults: (1) unintentional injuries and violence; (2) tobacco use; (3) alcohol and other drug use; (4) sexual behaviors that contribute to unintended pregnancy and HIV/other STD's; (5) unhealthy dietary behaviors; and (6) physical inactivity plus overweight. YRBSS is a national school-based survey conducted by the Centers for Disease Control and Prevention (CDC) as well as state and local-based surveys conducted by education and health agencies. The 2004 report summarizes results from the national survey, 32 state surveys, and 18 local surveys, which were conducted from February to December 2003 among students in grades 9-12. For more information, visit: http://www.cdc.gov/HealthyYouth/yrbs/

Monitoring the Future Study [6]

Since its inception over 30 years ago, the Monitoring the Future (MTF) study has been an excellent tool for tracking substance use behaviors of adolescents through young adulthood. Funded by the National Institute of

Drug Abuse (NIDA) and awarded to the University of Michigan, the annual survey consists of a nationally representative sample of approximately 50,000 8th-, 10th-, and 12th-grade student in about 400 middle schools and high schools. After graduation, annual follow-up questionnaires are mailed for a number of years. MTF is a study of behaviors, attitudes, and values of secondary school students, college students, and young adults in the United States. Additional information can be found at: http://www.m onitoringthefuture.org

While there is debate as to whether parents or peers have more influence on smoking (especially in late adolescence), parenting behaviors can have direct and indirect effects on smoking by influencing affiliation with smoking peers [9]. In other words, parent behaviors can act as a protective factor against smoking by limiting the number of friends who smoke. As such, this chapter will focus on parental behaviors and how they can influence their child's decision to smoke.

Specific behaviors that contribute to reducing an adolescent's risk for smoking include parental involvement, monitoring, and expressing expectations not to smoke [9, 10]. Adolescents who have parents with a more authoritative parenting style, characterized by parental support and control, are about half as likely to smoke as adolescents of parents with less-authoritative parenting styles [11, 12].

A parent's smoking status is also related to their children smoking as adolescents [13, 14]. In the adult population, cigarette smoking estimates are highest for American Indians/Alaska Natives (33.4 percent), followed by whites (22.2 percent), those with a General Education Development (GED) diploma (39.6 percent) or 9–11 years of education (34 percent), and adults who live below the poverty level (29.1 percent) [15].

A study conducted by Lawlor and colleagues [13] examined early life predictors of smoking among a birth cohort of Australian youth. They found that children with mothers who smoked throughout their pregnancy were 1.40 times more likely to smoke than mothers who never smoked during pregnancy.When the children were 14 years old, those with mothers who currently smoked were 1.57 times more likely to smoke than those whose mothers who did not smoke [13]. This finding may in part be due to unintentional cues a parent can give their child which subsequently encourages them to smoke. There is some evidence indicating that smoking-related prompting (e.g., asking child to buy cigarettes or asking child to light a cigarette) is correlated with adolescent smoking [16]; however, findings have been inconsistent as that relationship was no longer present at the 1-year follow-up [17]. As mentioned earlier, parental behavior can be a protective factor for smoking by limiting the number of smoking friends [9]. Conversely, adolescents with parents who smoke often have more friends who smoke as well [18].

Peterson et al. (2005) followed a cohort of more than 3,000 students from the 3rd to 12th grade to investigate the influence of smoking for children with two parents vs. one parent vs. no parents who smoke [14]. Parental smoking status was assessed when the children were in third grade and results were used to predict the child's smoking status by the time they were in 12th grade. Researchers found that, compared to children who had no smoking parents, those with only one smoking parent were 1.90 times more likely to smoke by the 12th grade and those with two smoking parents were 2.65 times more likely to smoke [14]. Even when comparing two versus one smoking parent, children with two smoking parents were 1.39 times more likely to smoke than if only one parent smoked. These finding demonstrate the extent to which parents' smoking behavior can influence their children to smoke and is a point that should be emphasized when educating parents in smoking prevention programs. Parents who smoke are encouraged to quit while their children are young. Nevertheless, there are measures that smoking parents can take to reduce their child's risk of smoking.

Research has provided some evidence that children of smoking parents have lower rates of smoking when parents communicate strong anti-smoking messages and establish household smoking ban rules [7, 11, 19, 20]. Sargent and Dalton (2001) reported that the effect of parental disapproval of smoking was stronger than the effect of parent smoking; and the effect of parental disapproval was equally strong for parents who smoked as for parents who did not smoke. Although other studies have not been able to find an association between reduction in adolescent smoking and parental attitudes among parents who smoke [10], this conflict may be due to differences in study design and methodology. For parents who decide to quit smoking, their child's odds of daily smoking have been shown to be reduced by 39% [21]. Generally, the messages parents deliver to their children about smoking have strong influences on their decision to smoke, whether the parents themselves smoke or not.

In summary, parental behaviors can have direct and indirect influences on adolescent smoking. Parenting style (i.e., more authoritative) can act as a protective factor by limiting the number of friends an adolescent has who smoke; but at the same time, parent behaviors can potentially increase the number of friends who smoke, such as when the parents themselves smoke [9, 11, 12]. Parents should be encouraged to quit smoking, as well as be given the proper guidance and resources to do so. While an adolescent's chance of refraining from smoking is increased when their parents are nonsmokers, there are measures *all* parents can take to increase their child's likelihood of living a smoke-free life. These are, for example: communicating strong anti-smoking messages/disapproval for smoking, parental involvement and monitoring, and establishing household smoking bans [9, 10, 19, 22].

Parent-Focused Adolescent Smoking Interventions

The previous section highlighted parental behaviors that can influence adolescent smoking (e.g., parenting style, anti-smoking communication, establishing household smoking bans, etc.); however, several questions still remain: What do parents know about preventing their children from smoking? Is what they *know* different from what they practice at home? Are family/parent-focused adolescent smoking interventions even feasible?

To speak to the latter, Guyll and colleagues (2004) followed 373 families participating in one of two randomized interventions and found that these family-focused interventions influenced alcohol only or both alcohol and tobacco index trajectories for adolescents. Students were followed from the 6th to 10th grade and the interventions were not designed for at-risk populations. From their results, investigators concluded that developing universal preventive interventions was feasible and could offer comparable benefits to all families [23].

More evidence that family-based interventions can be successful comes from a collection of model programs available through the Substance Abuse and Mental Health Services Administration (SAMHSA). Model programs, which are reviewed by the National Registry of Evidence-based Programs and Practices (NREPP) for strong scientific rigor, implementation, and evaluation, have an agreement with SAMHSA to provide materials, training, and assistance for nationwide implementation [24]. Model programs vary in study design and setting, including several programs that focus on family-based interventions (*see Research Highlight 2*).

When designing and developing programs for parents, it is beneficial to assess parents' knowledge on specific topics such as preventing adolescent smoking, as well as to examine how they apply their knowledge or attitudes. Sargent and Dalton (2001) concluded from their study that interventions designed to enhance a parent's self-efficacy in conveying and enforcing no-smoking policies could reduce adolescent smoking. However, even with the current findings linking parent behavior and adolescent smoking, more research is needed to identify whether there are gaps between what parents know about preventing their adolescent from smoking and what parents practice. This would give researches clues about parents' self-efficacy, or lack thereof, to carry out prevention strategies. With this understanding, researchers can design programs that focus on bridging this gap.

Information and guidelines available to parents about smoking prevention typically emphasize the importance of teaching children how to say no or walk away from cigarette offers, ensuring child involvement with sports or other extracurricular activities, talking with children about tobacco in the media, establishing household rules, and being aware of with whom and where children spend their time outside of the home (e.g., CDC, 2005). But what do parents themselves report knowing about adolescent smoking? And what do they practice? To answer these questions, analyses were done on the parent data from Healthy Generations, a study carried out by investigators at San Diego State University, Center for Behavioral and Community Health (1998-2002).

RESEARCH HIGHLIGHT 2

Below are two examples of successful family-based model programs that target adolescent substance use and are available for dissemination through the Substance Abuse and Mental Health Services Administration (SAMHSA). For more information on these programs and other model programs, visit http://modelprograms.samhsa.gov/

Family Matters [25, 26]

Family Matters is a home-based program designed to prevent tobacco and alcohol use in children age 12 to 14. The program is delivered through four booklets mailed to the home and includes follow-up telephone calls to the parents by health educators. The booklets are designed to get families to consider general family characteristics and family tobacco- and alcohol-use attitudes and other characteristics that can influence adolescent substance use, including: adult supervision and support; rule-setting and monitoring; family communication, attachment, and time together; education encouragement; family/adult substance use; substance availability; peer attitudes; and media orientation toward substance use.

To evaluate program effects, follow-up interviews were conducted at 3 and 12 months after receiving the Family Matters program. Adolescent who received the Family Matters program were 1.4 times less likely to have smoked cigarettes and 1.3 times less likely to have used alcohol compared to adolescents who did not receive the program.

Creating Lasting Family Connections (CLFC) [27]

CLFC is a comprehensive family strengthening, substance abuse, and violence prevention curriculum that has demonstrated that youth and families in high-risk environments can be assisted to become strong, healthy, and supportive people. The program has shown significant increases in resistance to the onset of substance use and reduction in use of alcohol and other drugs for children age 11 to 15. CLFC provides parents and children with strong defenses against environmental risk factors by teaching appropriate skills for personal growth, family enhancement, and interpersonal communication, including refusal skills for both parents and youth.

Adolescents who received the CLFC program had delayed onset of substance use. Their parents had increased knowledge about substance use and increased parental involvement in setting rules about substance use compared to those who did not receive the program.

Healthy Generations

The Healthy Generations study aims to examine parental influences on adolescent smoking and potential intervention approaches [16, 17, 28]. In the following analyses, we will describe results from the Healthy Generations study at one-year follow-up as they relate to parent knowledge about adolescent smoking, techniques parents report using to prevent tobacco use, and information parents provided that might be useful in developing smoking prevention programs aimed at parents.

Parents and students were recruited from lower to lower-middle income communities with a high concentration of Latinos, near the California/Mexico border. Approximately 10,500 recruitment letters and active consent forms, in both English and Spanish, were distributed to all 7th and 8th grade students in the three junior high and seven middle schools in the participating district, inviting them to participate in a cross-sectional study. Only students with signed parent consent forms and assent forms were included in the study. Additional information on the methodology of the Health Generations study, including survey development, test-retest reliability results and other psychometric characteristics, has been published elsewhere [16, 17, 29].

A total of 5,908 signed parent consent forms were returned.Of the returned signed consent forms, 1805 parents voluntarily provided phone numbers and indicated interest in participating in the study.Between January and July 2000, researchers attempted to contact 723 parents who had been identified as smokers by their child. We were unable to complete 431 (60%) interviews due to disconnected or wrong numbers (140), refusal to participate (141), and non-eligibility due to non-smoking status (196). A total of 292 (40%) parent interviews were completed.

Students in the study completed a paper-and-pencil survey, during school time, which included questions about demographic characteristics, including gender, ethnicity, smoking status, acculturation, familism, and parental smoking-related prompting behaviors. A similar questionnaire was developed to collect information over the telephone from smoking parents of the participating students, including self-reported parental smoking-related prompting behaviors, familism, acculturation, and types of tobacco prevention activities in which they might engage.

Tobacco-related questions were based on the California Tobacco Survey and assessed current and past 30 days tobacco use. Ten prompting questions were developed by the researchers to assess the level of parent prompting [16].Tobacco-related beliefs were measured using 8-items.Participants rated how much they agreed with a statement on a 5-point likert-type scale (1, agree to 5, disagree). For example: "It is harmful for kids to have an occasional cigarette" and "Smoking causes cancer". There were also five questions to assess parent exposure to anti-smoking messages on television, billboards or big signs, posters or pamphlets, newspaper or magazines, or the radio, and seven asking parents about the types of tobacco prevention activities in which they might participate. Participants indicated how likely they were to participate in specific intervention activities (e.g., read a pamphlet about smoking with their child or watch a video). Five items were used to measure familism which describes shared core values and beliefs that place high value on family unity and cohesiveness [16]. Finally, a language-based measure was used to assess acculturation for Latinos only [16]. A more detailed description of the broader Healthy Generations student and parent survey measures is reported elsewhere [17, 28, 30]. This analysis focuses on the parent telephone interviews that were conducted between the initial student survey and the one year student follow-up survey.

After the one year follow-up, one group of six parents participated in a focus group to further investigate potential smoking interventions. Results of this focus group were supplemented with information from 20 structured telephone interviews conducted with volunteers from the large pool of parents who had previously consented to participate in study activities. A random sample of telephone numbers from all parents were called until 20 interviews were completed. The focus group/telephone interview questionnaire included 13 questions regarding parent knowledge as it pertains to adolescent smoking, what parents do to discourage or prevent their children from smoking, types of smoking prevention programs that would facilitate parent participation, and barriers that prevent parents from interacting with their children. These questions were analyzed using simple descriptive statistics (i.e., percentages).

Among the 292 parents who participated in the broader study, the average parent age was 40 years (range 23-62). Sixty-seven percent of the smoking parents were female, and 51% were Latino. Fifty-seven percent were born in the U.S., 33% were born in Mexico, and 10% were born elsewhere, predominantly in the Philippines. Sixty-six percent were married or living with a partner. Fifty-one percent had a high-school diploma or general education degree. Forty-two percent of the families had more than two children. Eighty-three percent of the smoking parents were employed at the time of the survey. The median household monthly income was between $2200-2599. The mean families m score for parents (on a 4 point scale, low to high) was 3.3 (SD = .46), and the mean acculturation score for Latino parents (5 point scale, low to high) was 2.6 (SD = 1.04), a significantly lower score than that of their children (p = .000).Sixty-six percent of the parents reported "daily" smoking.

Telephone interviews revealed that the majority of parents reported that they discouraged their children from smoking by talking to them about the harmful effects of smoking on the body (75%). Ninety percent report having a household smoking ban (i.e., no one smokes in the house/must go outside). Other methods used by parents include setting a good example by not smoking themselves (25%) and showing their children television ads or pictures (25%).

When parents were asked to describe other types of factors that could discourage adolescents from smoking, 35% percent mentioned extracurricular activities (e.g., sports, church, and school). Similarly, when asked to describe other types of factors that could encourage children to smoke, 30% said not paying enough attention to the children or working too much. All parents (100%) reported that parents who smoke themselves may encourage smoking.

In spite of what parents know about discouraging their children from smoking, only 10% report actively keeping their children occupied with sports, trying to find ways to spend more time with them, teaching them to say no when offered a cigarette, and knowing who their friends are and how they spend time outside the home. Additionally, 10% or less of parents report expressing the following about smoking: it will affect their future negatively, it could lead to other types of drugs/addictions, saying they don't approve of smoking, they should focus on better things rather than smoking, it is harmful to others as well, and it can affect athletic abilities.

When parents were asked about characteristics of smoking prevention programs that would make it easier for them to participate, approximately half of the parents specified having a short program at the child's school, after classes, with parents separate from children, and having childcare available. Parents also reported that as part of a program, they would: read pamphlets about smoking with their child (45%), listen to a short audio tape about smoking issues (45%), watch a video (50%), attend meetings at the child's school (35%), accept a telephone call from a community health advisor (25%), and/or access the internet to find information on smoking (35%).Most of the parents who reported that they would do these activities, also said they would do them on more than just one occasion.

Seventy percent of parents said they would be motivated to participate in a prevention program because of a desire to learn more about adolescent smoking, tactics or techniques they can use with their children, and how to build communication skills. However, the biggest barrier reported by parents, which keeps them from being able to do activities with their children, is lack of time due to work (60%).

Implications: The Gap between What Parents Know and What Parents Practice

The Healthy Generations study aimed to describe parents' knowledge about adolescent smoking, techniques parents report using to prevent tobacco use, and potential intervention methods. Telephone interviews revealed that the majority of parents discouraged their children from smoking by talking to them about its harmful effects on the body and by having a household smoking ban. Parents also discouraged their children from smoking by setting a good example by not smoking themselves and by showing them television ads or pictures.

Parents reported knowing that extracurricular activities could help discourage a child from smoking, however few mention involving their children in sports for this purpose. The same is true for spending more time with their children. That is, while parents mention these factors as a way of preventing smoking, few report spending more time with their children, knowing who their friends are, or knowing how they spend their time outside the home.

These examples highlight the gap between what parents know about preventing smoking and what parents actually practice with their children. It may be that parents do not feel they are able to employ these techniques or, perhaps, there is just not enough time. Lack of time due to work is the biggest barrier reported by parents, which keeps them from being able to do activities with their children. While the amount of time a parent has to spend with their children is a difficult factor on which to intervene, the way in which a parent uses their free time may be a subject worth exploring. Increasing a parent's self-efficacy to participate in activities aimed at preventing smoking may encourage parents to use their free time towards such activities. Enhancing a parent's self-efficacy, in this way, could help reduce an adolescent's risk of smoking [20]. As one parent suggests:

> First, talk to [your] children, explain to them why they shouldn't smoke. Tell them about the illnesses that cigarettes cause and that they can kill. Keep them busy, for example, with activities in the library or in sports. Keep them away from kids that smoke. Keep a closer eye on them in and out the house. Know who they talk to on the phone, know their friends.

In addressing the lack of time parents report in being able to do activities with their children, exploring optimal conditions or characteristics of an intervention program is important in recruiting and retaining parents to participate. In this study, we found that parents would be motivated to participate in a prevention program because of a desire to learn more about adolescent smoking, tactics or techniques parents can use with their children, and how to build communication skills. Short programs that are located at the child's school seem to appeal to most parents, especially if childcare is provided. In addition, parents report willingness to watch videos, read pamphlets, search the internet, and accept health advisor phone calls as part of an intervention program.

A limitation of the present study is its relatively small sample size (n=20). The parents who chose to participate in the telephone interview (or who were able to be reached by phone) may be different from the larger pool of parents who consented to participate in the Healthy Generations study. Namely, these participants may already know more about adolescent smoking and/or are more involved with their children, for example. The results may, additionally, be specific to our population since the majority of parents and children in the study were Latino. Despite these limitations, the information obtained from this study points towards the need for further investigation on how parents can be involved in preventing adolescent smoking.

The findings from this study provide some evidence that a gap does exist between what parents know about preventing their children from smoking and what parents actually practice (i.e., what techniques they use). There is an abundance of evidence linking parent behavior and adolescent smoking, however future research on factors that can help facilitate implementation of smoking prevention strategies by parents is important for developing parent-related program components to reduce incidence and prevalence of adolescent smoking. Identifying the barriers parents face in being able to do activities with their children and in being able to participate in prevention programs are also important issues that should help inform the development/design of family-oriented adolescent smoking interventions. Overall, including parents in adolescent smoking prevention programs can have a great impact on reducing the risk of smoking and, therefore, preventing future disease of adolescents.

SOCIOECOLOGICAL INFLUENCES ON ADOLESCENT SMOKING

Parental influences have considerable impact on an adolescent's decision to smoke; and while these factors will continue to have strong influences, there has been a shift in the approach to health-risk behaviors, including tobacco use, from an individual and/or single-context focused approach to a more comprehensive, multilevel influence perspective. This includes, for example, working with peers, schools, and communities. An ecological framework, along with its theoretical underpinnings, has guided interest in incorporating multilevel intervention approaches to behaviors such as smoking, eating, and physical activity [31, 32].

New research has provided support for the push towards examining adolescent behavior in multiple social contexts, such that there is evidence for adolescents' family, peer, school, and neighborhood social contexts contributing both directly and indirectly to smoking involvement [33]. An example of current research examining multiple factors contributing to adolescent smoking is seen in the study, The Context of Adolescent Substance Use (Context Study), conducted at the University of North Carolina at Chapel Hill (*see Research Highlight 3*).

RESEARCH HIGHLIGHT 3

The Context of Adolescent Substance Use [33, 37-40]

Funded by the National Institute on Drug Abuse, the Context Study is designed to measure social contexts using multiple sources of information and innovative approaches. Contextual analyses of adolescent substance use comprises four main components: 1) a general population sample of adolescents who were identified by school enrollment and surveyed in school every six months for a total of five assessments, 2) a simple random sample of parents of the adolescents who were surveyed annually by telephone for a total of three assessments, 3) social network analysis of school networks based on friendship nominations collected in the school surveys, and 4) geocoding of all adolescent and parent addresses to allow linkage of the addresses to U.S. Census tracts and block groups.

In its transition from the last wave of data collection to the analysis stages of research, this study has already found some important relationships across multiple levels influencing adolescent health behavior and will likely reveal even more information about the context of adolescent substance use. Information stemming from this study has enabled researchers to examine peer network factors that predict trajectories of adolescent smoking, drinking and marijuana use and the social context, including family, friends, school, and neighborhood contexts, of smoking and drinking involvement.

Several reviews of the literature on youth smoking prevention have concluded that approaches directed at multiple levels of influence, such as media campaigns, community interventions, and policy change, are promising and warrant more attention [8, 34, 35]. One example of a successful approach involving the media is the "Truth Campaign", which has been found to change adolescents' beliefs and attitudes towards the tobacco industry [36]. As such, it is worth noting that targeting parental influences on adolescent smoking can ultimately become part of a larger, comprehensive prevention effort. In designing interventions aimed at adolescent smoking, the understanding of how several social and environmental contexts work both individually and together as influences will likely lead to the development of promising prevention programs.

CONCLUSION

In this chapter, we have established the importance of adolescent smoking as a public health priority. More than 6 million adolescents who smoke will die of tobacco-related illness as adults-- an addiction that remains the leading preventable cause of death in the United States [1]. Efforts to prevent adolescents from smoking should begin with younger age groups, as many of today's adult smokers began in adolescence; and many of the factors that influence adolescent smoking exert their effect beginning in childhood. Prevention programs that include parent-related components can help reduce an adolescent's risk of smoking, since a parent's own smoking pattern, parenting style, anti-smoking message communication, parental involvement, and establishment of household smoking bans can influence an adolescent's decision to smoke [9-12, 16, 19].

The Healthy Generations study provides evidence that a gap exists between what parents know about preventing their children from smoking and what parents actually practice. We have seen that the majority of parents discourage their children from smoking by talking to them about its harmful effects on the body and by having a household smoking ban, but few parents report spending more time with their children, knowing who their friends are, knowing how they spend their time outside the home, or teaching them to say no when offered a cigarette. Identifying the barriers that parents face are important issues that should also help inform the development of parent-oriented adolescent smoking prevention interventions. Short programs that are located at the child's school seem to appeal to parents, especially if childcare is provided, and most parents report willingness to watch videos, read pamphlets, search the internet, and accept health advisor phone calls as part of an intervention program.

Overall, parental influences have considerable impact on an adolescent's decision to smoke. In thinking about prevention, we should recognize the shift in the approach to health-risk behaviors from an individual and/or single-context focused approach to more comprehensive, multilevel strategies. As such, it is worth noting that targeting parental influences on adolescent smoking can ultimately become part of a larger picture-- that is, part of a comprehensive multilevel prevention effort. In designing interventions aimed at smoking prevention, we should work to understand how several social and environmental contexts work both individually and together as influences on smoking initiation. Such efforts will likely lead to the development of promising prevention programs and, consequently, can positively influence both the short- and long-term health outcomes of adolescents.

ACKNOWLEDGMENTS

Thanks to Dr. Susan Ennett for comments on this chapter.

REFERENCES

[1]   U.S. Department of Health and Human Services (USDHHS). *The Health Consequences of Smoking: A Report by Surgeon General.* Atlanta, GA: USDHHS, Centers for Disease Control and Prevention, National Center for Chronic Disease and Prevention and Health Promotion, Office on Smoking and Health, 2004.

[2]   Grunbaum JA, Kann L, Kinchen S, Ross J, Hawkins J, Lowry R, Harris WA, McManus T, Chyen D, Collins J. Youth Risk Behavior Surveillance-- United States, 2003. *Morbidity and Mortality Weekly Report* 2004; 53:1-96.

[3]   Centers for Disease Control and Prevention (CDC). Tobacco Use and the Health of Young People. Division of Adolescent and School Health: *www.cdc.gov/HealthyYouth/ Tobacco*, 2004. Accessed February 28, 2006.

[4]   Engels RCME, Hale WW, Noom M, de Vries H. Self-efficacy and emotional adjustment as precursors of smoking in early adolescence. *Substance Use and Misuse* 2005; 40:1883-1893.

[5]   Lindsay GB, Rainey J. Psychosocial and Pharmacologic Explanation of Nicotine's "Gateway Drug" Function. *The Journal of School Health* 1997; 67:123-126.

[6]   Johnston LD, O'Malley PM, Bachman JG, Schulenberg JE. Monitoring the Future national results on adolescent drug use: Overview of key findings, 2005. *National Institute of Health, Bethesda, MD: National Institute of Drug Abuse* 2006 (in press).

[7]   Turner L, Mermelstein R, Flay B. Individual and contextual influences on adolescent smoking. *Annals of the New York Academy of Science* 2004; 1021:175-197.

[8]   Backinger CL, Fagan P, Matthews E, Grana R. Adolescent and young adult tobacco prevention and cessation: current status and future directions. *Tobacco Control* 2003; 12:46-53.

[9]   Simons-Morton B, Chen R, Abroms L, Haynie DL. Latent growth curve analysis of peer and parental influences on smoking progression among early adolescents. *Health Psychology* 2004; 23:612-621.

[10] Andersen MR, Leroux BG, Marek PM, Peterson AV, Kealey KA, Sarason IG. Mothers' attitudes and concerns about their children smoking: do they influence kids? *Preventive Medicine* 2002; 34:198-206.

[11] Jackson C. Perceived legitimacy of parental authority and tobacco and alcohol use during early adolescence. *Journal of Adolescent Health* 2002; 31:425-432.

[12] Pierce JP, Distefan JM, Jackson C, White MM, Gilpin EA. Does tobacco marketing undermine the influence of recommended parenting in discouraging adolescents from smoking? *American Journal of Preventive Medicine* 2002; 23:73-81.

[13] Lawlor DA, O'Callaghan MJ, Mamun AA, Williams GM, Bor W, Najman JM. Early life predictors of adolescent smoking: findings from the Mater-University study of pregnancy and its outcomes. *Paediatric and Perinatal Epidemiology* 2005; 19:377-87.

[14] Peterson AVJ, Leroux BG, Bricker J, Kealey KA, Marek PM, Sarason IG, Andersen MR. Nine-year prediction of adolescent smoking by number of smoking parents. *Addictive Behaviors* 2005; In press (Epub ahead of print).

[15] Centers for Disease Control and Prevention (CDC). Cigarette smoking among adults--United States, 2004. *Morbidity and Mortality Weekly Report* 2005; 54:112-1124.

[16] Laniado-Laborin R, Woodruff SI, Candelaria JI, Sallis JF. Parental prompting and smoking among Latino youth. *Ethnicity and Disease* 2002; 12:508-516.

[17] Woodruff SI, Laniado-Laborin R, Candelaria JI, Villasenor A, Sallis JF. Parental prompts as risk factors for adolescent trial smoking: Results of a prospective cohort study. *Addictive Behaviors* 2004; 29:1869-1873.

[18] Engels RCME, Vitaro F, Blokland EDE, de Kemp R, Scholte RHJ. Influence and selection processes in frienships and adolescent smoking behaviour: the role of parental smoking. *Journal of Adolescence* 2004; 27:531-544.

[19] Conley TC, Siegel M, Winickoff J, Biener L, Rigotti NA. Household smoking bans and adolescents' perceived prevalence of smoking and social acceptability of smoking. *Preventive Medicine* 2005; 41:349-356.

[20] Sargent JD, Dalton M. Does parental disapproval of smoking prevent adolescents from becoming established smokers? *Pediatrics* 2001; 108:1256-1262.

[21] Bricker JB, Leroux BG, Andersen MR, Rajan KB, Peterson AV. Parental smoking cessation and children's smoking: mediation by antismoking actions. *Nicotine and Tobacco Research* 2005; 7:501-509.

[22] Centers for Disease Control and Prevention (CDC). Parents—Help Keep Your Kids Tobacco-Free. Tobacco Information and Prevention Source (TIPS). *http://www.cdc.gov /tobacco/educational_materials/*, 2005. Accessed February 28, 2006.

[23] Guyll M, Spoth RL, Chao W, Wickrama KA, Russell D. Family-focused interventions: evaluating parental risk moderation of substance use trajectories. *Journal of Family Psychology* 2004; 18:293-301.

[24] Substance Abuse and Mental Health Services Administration (SAMHSA). Website: *http://modelprograms.samhsa.gov/*. Accessed February 28, 2006.

[25] Bauman KE, Foshee V, Ennett ST, Hicks K, Pemberton M. Family Matters: a family-directed program designed to prevent adolescent tobacco and alcohol use. *Health Promotion Practice* 2001; 2:81-96.

[26] Ennett ST, Bauman KE, Pemberton M, Foshee V, Chuang YC, King TS, Koch GG. Mediation in a family-directed program for prevention of adolescent tobacco and alcohol use. *Preventive Medicine* 2001; 33:333-346.

[27] Johnston K, al. e. Reducing alcohol and other drug use by strengthening community, family, and youth resiliency: An evaluation of the Creating

Lasting Connections Program. *Journal of Adolescent Research* 1996; 11:36-67.

[28] Candelaria JI, Holub CK, Woodruff SI, Laniado-Laborin R, Sallis JF. *Smoking-Related Prompting Behaviors among Parents of Latino Adolescents: Identifying Potential Methods for Intervention.* (under review).

[29] Laniado-Laborin R. Parental Prompting as a Risk Factor for Smoking in Adolescents. Editor, Kane MJ. *Contemporary Issues in Parenting.* Hauppauge, NY: Nova Publishers, 2005.

[30] Laniado-Laborin R, Candelaria JI, Villasenor A, Woodruff SI, Sallis JF. Concordance between parental and children's reports of parental smoking prompts. *CHEST Journal* 2004; 125:429-434.

[31] Bronfenbrenner U. Toward an experimental ecology of human development. *American Psychologist* 1977:513-531.

[32] Sallis JF, Owen N. *Ecological models of health behavior.* In Glanz, K, Lewis, F M, Rimer, B K. *Health behavior and health education: theory, research, and practice.* San Francisco: Jossey-Bass, 2002.

[33] Ennett ST. The social ecology of adolescent smoking and drinking involvement. 2006; Under Review.

[34] Corbett KK. Susceptibility of youth to tobacco: a social ecological framework for prevention. *Respiration Physiology* 2001; 128:103-118.

[35] Lantz PM, Jacobson PD, Warner KE, Wasserman J, Pollack HA, Berson J, Ahistrom A. Investing in youth tobacco control: a review of smoking prevention and control strategies. *Tobacco Control* 2000; 9:47-63.

[36] Hershey JC, Niederdeppe J, Evans WD, Nonnemaker J, Blahut S, Holden D, Messeri P, Haviland ML. The theory of "truth": how counterindustry campaigns affect smoking behavior among teens. *Health Psychology* 2005; 24:22-31.

[37] Bauman KE, Faris R, Ennett ST, Hussong A, Foshee V. Adding valued data to social network measures: Does it add to associations with adolescent substance use? *Social Networks* in press.

[38] Ennett ST, Bauman KE, Hussong A, Farris R, Foshee V, DuRant RH, Cai L. The peer context of adolescent substance use: Findings from social network analysis. *Journal of Research on Adolescence* in press.

[39] Ennett ST, Faris R, Hipp J, Foshee V, Bauman KE, Hussong A, Cai L. Smoking involvement and friendship patterns from middle to high school. Invited paper. *Applications of Social Network Analysis to Prevention of Substance Use and Deliquency.* Pennsylvania State College, PA, 2005.

[40] Foshee V, Ennett ST, Bauman KE, Granger DA, Benefield T, Suchindran C, Hussong AM, Karriker-Jaffe KJ, DuRant RH. A test of biosocial models of alcohol and cigarette involvement. *Journal of Early Adolescence* in press.

In: Substance Abuse among Adolescents   ISBN: 978-1-61122-933-2
Editor: Isabelle M. Giordano   © 2011 Nova Science Publishers, Inc.

Chapter 2

CROSS-CULTURAL PARENT-CHILD RELATIONS: THE ROLE OF PARENTAL MONITORING IN YOUTH'S SUBSTANCE ABUSE BEHAVIORS IN HUNGARY AND THE UNITED STATES

Bettina F. Piko[1] and Kevin M. Fitzpatrick[2]
[1] University of Szeged, Hungary
[2] University of Arkansas, USA

ABSTRACT

Adolescence is an important development time when there is a significant restructuring in youth's social networks and support systems. A number of studies emphasize the negative role that peer groups play in determining youth's substance use, while still other studies find that youth substance use can be mediated by parental attitudes, family connectedness and monitoring. The main goal of the present study is to explore some of these associations in two different cultural settings. Data were collected among middle and high school students (ages 11-20 years) in Southern Hungary (N = 1240) and students (ages 10-19) living in a mid-sized urban area in Central Alabama, U.S. (N = 1525). The self-administered questionnaires were identical in both places and contained items that asked youth about their substance use (smoking, drinking, illicit drug use), and the parental/family influences in their life such as parental monitoring and parental attitudes towards substance use. Using multiple regression analyses in both samples, results suggest that parental monitoring (e.g., when parents know where their children are) is an important protective factor regardless of culture. Likewise, being beaten by a parent is an important universal risk factor. However, some differences may also be detected, e.g., parental attitudes towards substance use is an important influence only among Hungarian youth, while family structure is a significant predictor of substance use among US adolescents.

Keywords: parental monitoring, parental attitudes, youth substance use, cross-cultural comparison

INTRODUCTION

Adolescence is characterized by an increased experimentation with substance use, namely, smoking, drinking and drug use (Gilvarry, 2000). Among the influencing factors of adolescent substance use, the processes of social networks have always been in the focal point of research (Hawkins, Catalano and Miller, 1992; Piko, 2000; Poikolainen, 2002). Not surprisingly, social networks and social supports have been found to be key variables in predicting adolescents' health and health related behaviors (Frey and Röthlisberger, 1996). Adolescence is a period of life during which there is a restructuring of the social network and support systems (Aneshensel and Gore, 1991; Piko, 2000). During adolescence, youth begin to develop peer-oriented relationships while their link to parents undergoes dramatic changes as well. Although adolescence is definitely characterized by spending more time with peers and less with parents, the restructuring is not merely a question of quantitative change but qualitative change as well. Many researchers emphasize that parent-adolescent relations continue to serve as an adaptive function by providing a secure base for adolescents as they begin exploring new, peer based environments (Paterson, Pryor, and Field, 1995).

The enduring family socialization model suggests a consistent parental influence on adolescents' health related behavior, although parents sometimes may be unaware of the influence of their behaviors or parenting practices on children in this period of life (Christensen, 2004; Norton, Sivarajan-Froelicher, Waters, and Carrieri-Kohlman, 2003). Parenting style is based on two dimensions of parental practices, namely, control (that is, strictness, demandedness) and warmth (attachment, responsiveness, communication). In terms of adolescent development, the best outcomes tend to be those associated with the authoritative parenting style, when a parent is warm yet still expresses a moderate level of control (Radziszewska, Richardson, Dent, and Flay, 1996). This parenting style represents both demanding and responsive parental practices which appear to be protective against adolescent substance use as well (Jackson, Henriksen, and Foshee, 1998; Simons-Morton, Haynie, Crump, Eitel, and Saylor, 2001). In addition to parenting style, parental attitudes towards substance use, that is, approval or disapproval have been found to be a more important correlate of adolescent substance use than parental substance use (Piko, 2001; Sargent and Dalton, 2001).

Regarding adolescent substance use, one aspect of parent-child relations is the monitoring function. Parental monitoring consists of the knowledge of where and with whom youth spend their time with (Li, Feigelman, and Stanton, 2000). Thus, parental monitoring includes an active attempt to control youth (e.g., when parents set a curfew or they have rules established for letting them know where their children are). This function is closely connected with parenting practices, therefore, parental monitoring may serve as important protection not only against substance use but also against conduct problems (Deković, 1999). High parental monitoring and involvement have been found to be negatively associated with youth's substance use (Li, Stanton, and Feigelman, 2000; Steinberg, Fletcher, and Darling, 1994).

Another aspect of the parent-child relation is connectedness/attachment such as the utilization of emotional support, proximity, and the quality of affect. Harmony, closeness or support are the elements of parent-child relationships which are extraordinarily important in terms of the maintaining affective ties between parents and adolescents. These aspects are key elements in adolescent adjustment because despite the decreased frequency of interaction during the adolescent years they provide protection against youth's substance use and other problem behaviors (Vazsonyi, 2003). Adolescents with greater family togetherness score lower levels of depression and drug use (Field, Diego, and Sanders, 2002). In addition, adolescents with higher family bonds are less likely to have close friends involved in substance use (Bahr, Marcos, and Maughan, 1995). Another element in parent-child connectedness is the communication between them. Communicating well with parents, that is, talking about problems with them is associated with lower levels of substance use (Stronski, Ireland, Michaud, Narring, and Resnick, 2000). Another study also supports the idea that parents continue to exert an influential role even in late adolescent substance use (Wood, Read, Mitchell, and Brand, 2004). Other studies, however, suggest that in comparison with peer effects, the influences of parental monitoring and attachment to parents are relatively small if significant (Bahr, Hoffmann, and Yang, 2005). Therefore, further research is needed to interpret not only the relative but the absolute role of parental variables in understanding adolescent substance use.

Beyond parental practices, living in high risk families may also enhance the risk of adolescent substance use. Family life events and family structure may serve as risk factors in terms of adolescents' substance use. Children who experience family life events such as parental unemployment, divorce or separation are at an elevated risk to experience emotional and behavioral problems (Harland, Reijneveld, Brugman, Verloove-Vanhorick, and Verhulst, 2002). Domestic violence and being beaten by parents foster children's problem behavior (Formoso, Gonzales, and Aiken, 2000; Jaffee, Moffitt, Caspi, Taylor, and Arseneault, 2002). Another familial risk factor is the non-intact family structure when one or both parents are absent from the home (Ackerman, D'Eramo, Umylny, Schultz, and Izard, 2001). Family structure is particularly important in terms of problem behaviors of children living in economically disadvantaged or minority families (Fitzpatrick, 1997a).

Besides sociodemographics, cultural factors also may influence the frequencies of substance use and the role of these background variables. A number of cross-cultural studies report on the cultural differences in adolescent substance use (Steptoe and Wardle, 1992). Research documents, for example, that smoking is more frequent among European youth than their American counterparts (Brown, 2002). This is particularly true in case of Eastern European youth where smoking has a high rates both among adults and adolescents (Piko, Luszczynska, Gibbons, and Teközel, 2005). The differences in alcohol use is less significant, in addition, drug use is usually more common among American youth than European, particularly Eastern European youth (Piko and Fitzpatrick, 2001). There is much less research regarding the influencing factors of adolescent substance use and the specific roles of parenting practices and other familial variables. Based on previous findings, however, Vazsonyi (2003) raised an universal explanation for the role of family processes in adolescents' problem behavior with very few invariations across different cultures. Chen and colleagues argue that measures of parent-adolescent relationship (e.g., warmth or monitoring) are related to adolescent problem behavior in a highly similar fashion cross-culturally (Chen, Greenberger, Lester, Don, and Guo, 1998). Chirkov and Ryan (2001) explain this similarity by pointing out similar socialization goals and mechanisms to achieve them. Despite possible differences in concrete parenting behavior, parenting goals and practices seem to be rather universal (Rohner and Britner, 2002).

Since adolescence is a critical period of life in terms of further development, we should know more about the parent-child relationship. This is particularly important in the modern world when prolonged puberty has emerged bringing new challenges for adolescents' social network systems. Cross-cultural research definitely aids us in developing a better understanding of family processes during this period of life. Therefore, the main goal of the present study is to give an outline of parental and familial influences of adolescent substance use (namely, smoking, drinking and marijuana use) in two different cultural settings. First, the study is based on a data collection in a sample of American (Southern African-American) youth, and second, a sample of European (Southern Hungarian) youth. Previous findings suggest that socialization processes in European and American adolescents are somewhat different and in fact result in differences in their substance use and problem behaviors (Arnett and Jensen, 1994). In addition, studies also draw attention to the similarities in risk and protective stuctures of the influencing factors suggesting that despite any differences in the amount of problem behaviors, some universal tendencies in the background variables may be justified (Fitzpatrick, Piko and Wright, 2005; Piko, Fitzpatrick, and Wright, 2005). Using two samples from distinct cultural settings, we have the somewhat unique opportunity to detect possible differences and similarities in a number of parenting and familial factors influencing adolescent substance use.

METHODS

Samples

American Sample

The sample consists of 1,525 African-American middle and high school students from a single school district in central Alabama. The majority of the residents living in the school district are African-American (60%); over one-third (35%) are from families headed by a female with children under the age of 18; and over one-third are living below the poverty level. Of the sampled students, approximately 49% were males and the median age of the sample was 14 years of age (9th grade), age range: 10-19 years (Mean = 14.0 years, S.D. = 2.3 years). The 2001-2002 average daily attendance (ADA) for the middle and high schools in the system was 2,028 students. Student's participation in the study was voluntary, yielding a response rate of approximately 76%. After approval, written parental permission was obtained. In addition to those students who decided against participation (< 10%), the remaining students likely consisted of youth who were absent, suspended, or no longer attending school in the system.

Hungarian Sample

This sample consists of 1,240 middle and high school students (age range: 11-20 years) from seven schools in Szeged, a major metropolitan center of southern Hungary, where data collection was based on random selection of classes. The majority of residents living in Szeged are Caucasian (above 90%). Most students were from two-parent families (66.5%) or lived with a parent and a step-parent (10.8%), only 17.9% of them lived with their mother, 2.3% with their father and 2.5% with other relatives. Of the sampled students, 53% were males and the median age of the sample was 16 years of age (Mean = 15.6 years, S.D. = 2.1 years). Of the 1,500 questionnaires sent out (approximately 13% of the entire student population), 1,240 were returned, giving us a response rate of approximately 84%. Similar to the American sample, student participation was voluntary and confidentiality was emphasized, noting that the data used in the study were for research purposes only.

MEASURES

Three types of *substance use* were included in the analyses: smoking, drinking and marijuana use (Search Institute, 1998). Regarding the frequency of smoking, the following questions were asked: "How much in the past 30 days did you smoke cigarettes?" Response categories were the following: not at all (1), less than 1 a day (2), 1-5 cigarettes a day (3), 6-10 cigarettes a day (4), 11-20 cigarettes a day (5), more than pack a day (6). Regarding alcohol use, a similar question was asked: "How many times in the past 30 days did you drink alcohol (including beer, wine, wine coolers, rum, gin, wodka, whisky, etc.)?" Response categories in terms of drinking were never (1), once or twice (2), 3 to 9 times (3), 10 to 19 times (4), 20 to 39 times (5) and 40 or more times (6). Regarding drug use, the most common form, that is, marijuana use was measured: "How many times in the past 30 days did you smoke marijuana (pot, grass, blunt)?" Response categories were the following: none

(1), once or twice (2), 3 to 9 times (3), 10 to 19 times (4), 20 to 39 times (5), and 40 or more times (6).

Among the parental and familial factors, father's and mother's schooling, and family structure were included in the analyses as sociodemographics. A four-level classification of education was used to measure father and mother schooling: primary education = 1; apprenticeship = 2; high school level (General Certificate of Education in Hungary) = 3; and university or college degree = 4. Students were also asked about the family structure, that is, with whom do they live together most of the time? The variable was dichotomized reflecting parental absence/presence (Fitzpatrick, 1997b). In addition, various questions were asked about parenting practices (Ary, Duncan, Biglan, Metzler, Noell, and Smolkowski, 1999; Deković, 1999; Search Institute, 1998). Parental monitoring was measured by using two independent items. First, students were asked whether their parents typically set a curfew for them. Students were also asked whether their parents knew where they were when they were going out with friends. Both variables were coded from 0 = never set/never knew to 4 = always set/knew all the time.

Regarding family cohesion, students were asked the following question: "Thinking about Monday through Friday, how often do you come home after school and there is no adult at home?" Response categories were never (0), rarely (1), once a month (2), 2-4 times a week (3), and every day. In addition, students were asked about sharing a meal together as a family: "How often do you eat dinner with your family?" Responses were never (0), a few times (1), some of the time (2), most of the time (3), and all of the time (4).

As variables of family connectedness/attachment, students were asked how often they talked with their parents/guardians about their personal problems. This variable was coded as 0 = never, 1 = hardly ever, 2 = sometimes, 3 = most of the time and 4 = all of the time. In contrast with this variable, a family risk factor was also asked as a measure of parent-child conflict. Students were asked whether they had ever been beaten by a parent or adult living with them and those ordinal responses were 0 = never, 1 = once or twice, 2 = several times, 3 = alot of times, and 4 = all the time.

Finally, parental disapproval of substance use in general also was included: "How do you think your parents feel about substance use?" This variable was measured by a five-point scale which varied from strongly agree (1) to strongly disagree (5).

PROCEDURE

The data for both samples were collected between the academic years of 2000 and 2001. In both cases, questionnaires were self-administered under close supervision by classroom teachers. Teachers received training and a set of instructions outlining the administration of the survey, confidentiality, and procedures for responding to student's questions. Students filled out questionnaires during the class period. When finished, respondents returned them in sealed envelopes, which were then collected from the participating schools.

DATA ANALYSIS

For statistical analysis, SPSS 12.0 was used and the minimum level of significance was set at .05. The analysis begins with an examination of the descriptive statistics for the substance use variables and parental/familial factors. Student's t-tests and Chi-square tests were initially used to determine significant gender and sample differences. Multiple regression analyses were applied to explore the relative effects of parental and familial factors on the frequency of each type of substance use. Possible gender differences also were detected in the background variables. In addition, results of the two samples were examined separately to explore cross-cultural differences or similarities.

RESULTS

Figure 1 shows the smoking patterns among Hungarian and American youth. A significant difference exists showing more Hungarian students reported cigarette smoking (51%) compared to the frequencies of American youth (23.3%), particularly in terms of heavy smoking (p<.001 by Chi-square test). For example, the percentage of those reporting 6-10 cigarettes/day was 1.0% among American but 12.3% among Hungarian youth. The percentage of those smoking 11-20 cigarettes/day during the past month was 1.2% among Americans but 9.1% among Hungarian youth. Similar patterns may be noticed in terms of alcohol use (see Figure 2): 31.2% of American youth compared to 53% of Hungarian youth reported drinking during the past month (p<.001 by Chi-square test). However, the percentage of regular drinkers (more than 20 times/month) was nearly the same (2.2% among American and 2.4% among

Hungarian youth). In contrast to smoking and drinking, marijuana use was more common among American students: 18.8% of them reported using marijuana during the past 30 days in contrast to 6.5% of Hungarian youth (see Figure 3).

Table 1 provides detailed descriptive statistics for the samples broken by gender. Both gender and sample differences in parental and familial variables were calculated.

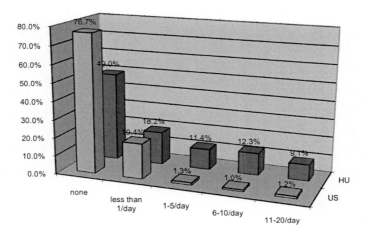

Figure 1. Smoking patterns among Hungarian and American youth

There were no significant gender differences in the frequencies of being beaten by a parent or family structure, although this latter variable shows rather large differences between samples. Among American youth, all variables of parental and familial factors show significant gender differences, that is, more girls than boys receive parental monitoring such as the setting of a curfew by parents and likewise girls report that they talk about problems more often with their parents. In the Hungarian sample, similar to their American counterparts, girls report more parental monitoring (e.g., when parents state a curfew and their parents know where they are) and talk more about problems with parents. However, in contrast with American youth, there were no significant gender differences in having dinner together, the presence of an adult at home after school or parental disapproval of substance use.

Table 1. Descriptive statistics by gender for parental and familial factors for Hungarian (n = 1,240) and American youth (n = 1,538)

	HUNGARIAN SAMPLE			AMERICAN SAMPLE		
	Boys	Girls	Gender significance	Boys	Girls	Gender significance
[a]Beaten by parent (Mean, S.D.)	1.4 (0.7)	1.5 (0.8)	N.S.	1.4 (0.8)	1.4 (0.8)	N.S.
[b]Family structure (%)+ Non-intact vs. Intact	30.9 69.1	36.8 63.2	N.S.	70.6 29.4	74.3 25.7	N.S.
[a]Parents set a curfew (Mean, S.D.)	2.8 (1.5)	3.4 (1.5)	p<.001	3.1 (1.5)	3.3 (1.5)	p<.05
[a]Parents know where their children are (Mean, S.D.)+	3.5 (1.3)	4.0 (1.1)	p<.001	3.9 (1.2)	4.3 (1.1)	p<.001
[a]Talking about problems with parents (Mean, S.D.)	2.9 (1.1)	3.4 (1.1)	p<.001	2.8 (1.3)	3.1 (1.3)	p<.001
[a]Eating together as a family (Mean, S.D.)	3.2 (1.2)	3.2 (1.2)	N.S.	3.6 (1.3)	3.4 (1.3)	p<.01
[a]Adult at home after school (Mean, S.D.)+	3.6 (1.8)	3.4 (1.9)	N.S.	2.8 (1.7)	2.6 (1.6)	p<.01
[a]Parental disapproval of substance use (Mean, S.D.)+	4.2 (0.9)	4.2 (0.9)	N.S.	3.6 (1.7)	3.9 (1.6)	p<.001

[a]ANOVA, [b]Chi-square test
+p<.01 for sample differences

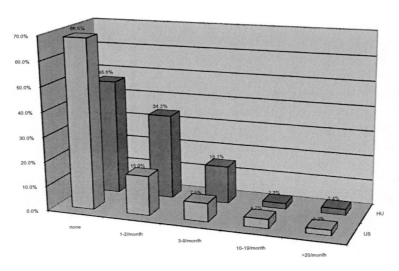

Figure 2. Drinking patterns among Hungarian and American youth

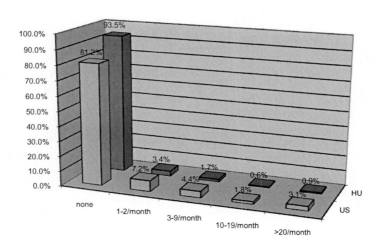

Figure 3. Marijuana use among Hungarian and American youth

Table 2. Standardized regression estimates for parental and other familial factors in predicting Hungarian youth's smoking (n = 1240)

	WHOLE	BOYS	GIRLS
Parental and other familial factors			
Father schooling	0.06[a]	0.01[a]	0.01[a]
Mother schooling	0.09	0.02	0.01
Family intactness	-0.04	-0.03	-0.06
Beaten by a parent	0.10***	0.10**	0.11*
Having dinner as a family	-0.01	-0.01	-0.02
Adult at home after school	-0.03	-0.08*	-0.02
Talking about problems with parents	-0.01	0.01	-0.01
Parents set a curfew	-0.14***	-0.16***	-0.10*
Parents know where the children are	-0.15***	-0.15***	-0.134**
Parental disapproval of substance use	-0.25***	-0.27**	-0.24***
Constant	1.308***	1.008**	1.422***
R^2	0.17***	0.18***	0.15***

One-tailed t-tests *$p < 0.05$; **$p < 0.01$; ***$p < 0.001$
[a]Standardized regression coefficients

In addition to differences in family structure between the samples (that is, a higher rate of non-intact families in the US sample), American adolescents report more parental monitoring (parents knowing where their children are), while Hungarian youth report a greater frequency of an adult's presence at home after school and greater parental disapproval of substance use.

Table 3. Standardized regression estimates for parental and other familial factors in predicting Hungarian youth's alcohol use (n = 1240)

	WHOLE	BOYS	GIRLS
Parental and other familial factors			
Father schooling	-0.01[a]	0.04[a]	-0.04[a]
Mother schooling	-0.01	-0.02	0.01
Family intactness	-0.01	-0.02	-0.05
Beaten by a parent	0.07**	0.07*	0.10*
Having dinner as a family	-0.02	0.01	-0.07
Adult at home after school	-0.02	-0.03	-0.01
Talking about problems with parents	-0.07*	-0.05	-0.04
Parents set a curfew	-0.20***	-0.22***	-0.15***
Parents know where the children are	-0.14***	-0.12**	-0.15***
Parental disapproval of substance use	-0.23***	-0.18***	-0.32***
Constant	2.179***	2.176**	1.965***
R^2	0.19***	0.14***	0.25***

One-tailed t-tests *$p < 0.05$; **$p < 0.01$; ***$p < 0.001$
[a]Standardized regression coefficients

Table 2 presents regression estimates of smoking among Hungarian youth in the whole sample and broken by gender subgroups. In each case, being beaten by a parent was a positive influence on smoking. Among the negative correlates, parental monitoring (setting a curfew and knowing where youth were) proved to be significant regardless of gender. In addition, those reporting a greater level of parental disapproval of substance use tended to smoke less.

Table 4. Standardized regression estimates for parental and other familial factors in predicting Hungarian youth's marijuana use (n = 1240)

	WHOLE	BOYS	GIRLS
Parental and other familial factors			
Father schooling	-0.01[a]	-0.03[a]	0.07[a]
Mother schooling	0.08*	0.12*	0.07
Family intactness	0.01	0.01	-0.03
Beaten by a parent	0.05	0.05	0.10*
Having dinner as a family	-0.02	-0.06	0.04
Adult at home after school	-0.01	-0.01	-0.03
Talking about problems with parents	-0.02	-0.03	-0.10*
Parents set a curfew	-0.11***	-0.09*	-0.12**
Parents know where the children are	-0.15***	-0.15***	-0.09*
Parental disapproval of substance use	-0.26***	-0.14***	-0.19***
Constant	0.262	0.278	0.001
R^2	0.09***	0.08***	0.12***

One-tailed t-tests *$p < 0.05$; **$p < 0.01$; ***$p < 0.001$
[a]Standardized regression coefficients

Table 5. Standardized regression estimates for parental and other familial factors in predicting American youth's smoking (n = 1538)

	WHOLE	BOYS	GIRLS
Parental and other familial factors			
Father schooling	-0.01[a]	-0.03[a]	-0.03[a]
Mother schooling	0.02	0.02	0.01
Family intactness	-0.07**	-0.07*	-0.06*
Beaten by a parent	0.11***	0.12***	0.09*
Having dinner as a family	-0.01	-0.07*	-0.05
Adult at home after school	-0.05	-0.02	-0.08*
Talking about problems with parents	-0.06*	-0.01	-0.09**
Parents set a curfew	0.01	0.01	0.03
Parents know where the children are	-0.18***	-0.18***	-0.16***
Parental disapproval of substance use	-0.02	-0.01	-0.05
Constant	0.792***	0.955***	0.587***
R2	0.07***	0.07***	0.07***

One-tailed t-tests *$p < 0.05$; **$p < 0.01$; ***$p < 0.001$
[a]Standardized regression coefficients

Table 3 presents regression estimates of alcohol use among Hungarian youth in similar groupings to the models specified in the earlier tables. Again, being beaten by a parent was a significant predictor. Among the negative influences, parental monitoring and parental disapproval of substance use predicted youth's drinking patterns.

Table 4 displays regression estimates of marijuana use among Hungarian youth. In addition to similar results, compared with the two previous types of substance use (that is, the role of parental monitoring and parental disapproval), some differences were detected. Among boys, there were no more factors acting as significant predictors. Among girls, however, being beaten by a parent was positive, while talking about problems with parents acted as a negative influence.

Table 5 presents regression estimates of smoking among American youth in the whole sample and broken into gender subgroups similar to the Hungarian sample in the earlier table 2. Similar to the results of the Hungarian sample, being beaten by a parent was a positive influence for both sexes. Among the negative influences, parents knowing where youth were and family intactness were signficant predictors for both boys and girls..

Table 6. Standardized regression estimates for parental and other familial factors in predicting American youth's alcohol use (n = 1240)

	WHOLE	BOYS	GIRLS
Parental and other familial factors			
Father schooling	0.02[a]	-0.02[a]	0.08*[a]
Mother schooling	-0.01	0.02	-0.05
Family intactness	-0.05*	-0.05	-0.05
Beaten by a parent	0.12***	0.13***	0.11**
Having dinner as a family	-0.05	-0.09*	-0.01
Adult at home after school	-0.07**	-0.03	-0.13***
Talking about problems with parents	-0.05	-0.01	-0.09**
Parents set a curfew	-0.07**	-0.11**	-0.02
Parents know where the children are	-0.15***	-0.10**	-0.19***
Parental disapproval of substance use	-0.03	-0.04	-0.02
Constant	1.153***	1.284**	1.005***
R^2	0.09***	0.09***	0.11***

One-tailed t-tests *p < 0.05; **p < 0.01; ***p < 0.001
[a]Standardized regression coefficients

Table 6 presents regression estimates of alcohol use among American youth in similar groupings to the earlier tables. As found in table 5, being beaten by a parent exerted a positive influence on increasing risk behavior. Among the negative influences, parents knowing where their children were proved to be a significant parental factor for both sexes. In addition, talking about problems with parents and the variable showing an adult's presence at home after school were significant predictors for girls. Among boys, having dinner together as a family and parental setting a curfew were significant predictors.

Table 7 displays regression estimates of marijuana use among American youth. Again, being beaten by a parent exerted a positive influence on risk behavior similar to other regression estimates for both American and Hungarian youth. Among the negative influences, parents knowing where the children were proved to be significant for both sexes. Setting a curfew and parental disapproval of substance use were significant predictors of marijuana use only for boys, talking about problems with parents and family intactness were predictors only for girls.

Table 7. Standardized regression estimates for parental and other familial factors in predicting American youth's marijuana use (n = 1240)

	WHOLE	BOYS	GIRLS
Parental and other familial factors			
Father schooling	-0.05*[a]	-0.06[a]	-0.04[a]
Mother schooling	0.03*	0.05	-0.03
Family intactness	-0.05*	-0.04	-0.08*
Beaten by a parent	0.10***	0.14***	0.05
Having dinner as a family	-0.01	-0.01	-0.04
Adult at home after school	-0.01	-0.01	-0.02
Talking about problems with parents	-0.04	-0.01	-0.08*
Parents set a curfew	-0.08**	-0.11**	-0.05
Parents know where the children are	-0.17***	-0.15***	-0.17***
Parental disapproval of substance use	-0.03	-0.08	-0.02
Constant	0.983***	0.833***	1.042***
R^2	0.07***	0.08***	0.08***

One-tailed t-tests *p < 0.05; **p < 0.01; ***p < 0.001
[a]Standardized regression coefficients

In addition to these specific differences between drugs, there were also important differences by samples in the amount of variation these models actually explained. Generally, explained variation was greater in the Hungarian samples in each of the substance use models. For example, in terms of smoking, the variations explained proved to be the following: 7% in American youth and 15-18% in Hungarian youth. Regarding alcohol use, it was 9-11% in American youth and 14-25% in Hungarian youth. The percentages were the following in case of marijuana use: 9-12% in Hungarian youth and 7-8% in American youth.

DISCUSSION

Research continues to analyze the background variables of adolescent substance use, particularly those related to youth's social network (Deković, 1999; Hawkins, Catalano, and Miller, 1992; Piko, 2000; Poikolainen, 2002). With tremendous restructuring of the social network and support systems during adolescence a strong influence on youth's lifestyle and health related behaviors has been documented (Frey and Rötlisberger, 1996; Aneshensel and Gore, 1991; Piko, 2000). While there are a number of studies investigating the role of peers, more research is needed to gain a better understanding of the role of parental practices and other familial factors in youth's substance use and problem behaviors (Vazsonyi, 2003). Thus, the main goal of the present study has been to investigate parental and familial influences on the adolescent risk-taking behaviors of smoking, drinking and marijuana use.

The current investigation adds to the literature on parent-adolescent relationship in several ways. First, the study examined various parental and familial factors such as parental monitoring, parental attitudes towards substance use and parent-child connectedness. Second, the study is based on a data collection of youth from two different cultural settings which provides us an opportunity to detect possible differences and similarities in a number of parenting and familial influences of adolescent substance use. The cross-cultural comparison helps us develop a better understanding of the universality versus cultural specificity of parental practices (Chen et al., 1998; Chirkov and Ryan, 2001; Rohner and Britner, 2002).

The most striking findings of our results are the following: 1) There are significant differences in both the frequencies of substance use and the kinds of parental practices; 2) the role of parenting practices in youth's substance use is quite similar in both cultural settings, and 3) although there are similarities in the structure of parental and familial factors which are dominant cross-culturally, some minor differences are observed.

The descriptive statistics show that smoking and drinking are more common among Hungarian while marijuana use is more common among American youth similar to previous studies (Brown, 2002; Piko et al., 2005; Steptoe and Wardle, 1992; Vazsonyi, 2003). Hungarian youth reported greater presence of an adult at home after school and more intact families as well as a greater parental disapproval of substance use. On the other hand, American youth stated that more parents knew where their children were. Being beaten by a parent showed gender differences in none of the samples while parental monitoring was more common among girls in both samples.

We included a number of parental and familial factors in the model explaining youth's substance use. All in all, these factors explain only a small amount of variations in the multivariate model. This is particularly true in case of the American sample (between 7 and 11% altogether) while the variations explained were greater in the analyses for the Hungarian sample (between 9 and 25% altogether). Previous studies also report that parental factors play little role in the development of adolescents' substance use as compared to peer groups effects (Ary et al., 1999; Piko, 2001; Simons-Morton et al., 2001). It seems to be, however, that parental and familial factors are more important determinants of Hungarian adolescents' substance use, particularly in terms of smoking and drinking.

Among the parental and familial factors, being beaten by a parent seems to be a universal positive influence regardless of gender or culture. Those who experience this type of parent-child conflict report higher levels of substance use similar to previous studies (Formoso, Gonzales, and Aiken, 2000; Jaffee et al., 2002). Likewise, a certain form of parental monitoring, that is, when the parents know where their children are, seems to exert a universal negative influence. The other form of parental monitoring, curfew setting by parents seems to be more important for Hungarian youth. This variable was a significant predictor of substance use among Hungarian youth in each case of substance use in both sexes. However, for American youth, this was only a significant predictor of boys' alcohol and drug use, in addition, the relationships that were observed were not as strong. Previous studies also have found that parental monitoring may serve as an important protection against adolescent substance use (Deković, 1999; Li, Feigelman, and Stanton, 2000; Li, Stanton, and Feigelman, 2000; Stenberg, Fletcher and Darling, 1994). The differences may be attributed to a more traditional parenting style found in Hungary (Vazsonyi, 2003).

Another difference in the structure of parental/familial influences lies in the role of family structure. In the Hungarian sample, more children reported living in an intact family and the family structure tended not to play a significant role in their substance use. In the American sample, however, more children live in a non-intact family and the family intactness may serve as a protection against their substance use. Other studies from the U.S. also report on the role of family structure, particularly for children living in economically disadvantaged or minority families (Ackerman et al., 2001; Fitzpatrick, 1997a). In contrast with this variable, parental disapproval seems to be an important influence for Hungarian youth. Another study from Hungary also reports on the importance of parental attitudes towards children's substance use (Piko, 2001). Parental attitudes are much more important determinant of children's substance use than parental behavior in contrast with peer behavior (Simons-Morton et al., 2001). For American youth, parental attitudes do not seem to make a difference.

Other types of parental practices such as talking about problems with parents, having dinner together as a family or the presence of an adult at home after school are more important for American youth. These variables represent certain aspects of family connectedness which may serve as a protection against adolescent substance use (Stronski et al., 2000; Vazsonyi, 2003). This is particularly noteworthing taking into account the high level of non-intact families in the U.S.

Our findings provide important evidence for the role of parental and familial factors in adolescent substance use (Wood et al., 2004). Despite the fact that these effects are relatively lower than those of peer groups, the parent-adolescent relations continue to provide a secure base for adolescents during this period of their development (Paterson, Pryor and Field, 1995). Due to the special characteristics of the samples (a sample of youth from an Eastern European country, and the African-American sample living in a low-income urban setting in the Southern US), the generalizibility of our findings may be limited. Some additional limitations also should be noted here. Because of the cross-sectional study design, our results cannot provide an explanatory (cause and effect) model for understanding externalizing problem behavior. Additionally, the current study of parental/familial influences is based on youth's self-reports. Although we should mention here that previous studies also recommend that studies of parent-child relationships should be based on children's self-reports which reflect their valid perceptions of parental monitoring (Gray and Steinberg, 1999).

As a summary, we think that our data make a valuable contribution toward a better understanding of youth substance use and the role(s) of parental/familial influences. Future studies should continue to examine the relative and absolute effects of parental/familial structure on adolescent substance use within the cross-cultural context. In addition, future research should also consider longitudinal study designs for a more comprehensive explanatory framework for understanding parent-child relationship and its consequences.

REFERENCES

Ackerman, B. P., D'Eramo, K. S., Umylny, L., Schultz, D., and Izard, C. E. (2001). Family structure and the externalizing behavior of children from economically disadvantaged families. *Journal of Family Psychology*, 15, 288-300.

Aneshensel, C. S., and Gore, S. (1991). Development, stress and role restructuring. Social transitions in adolescence. In J. Eckenrode (Ed.), *The social context of coping* (pp. 55-77). New York and London: Plenum Press.

Arnett, J. J., and Jensen, L. A. (1994). Socialization and risk behavior in two countries: Denmark and the United States. *Youth and Society*, 26, 3-20.

Ary, D. V., Duncan, T. E., Biglan, A., Metzler, C. W., Noell, J. W., and Smolkowski, K. (1999). Development of adolescent problem behavior. *Journal of Abnormal Child Psychology*, 27, 141-150.

Bahr, S. J., Hoffmann, J. P., and Yang, X. (2005). Parental and peer influences on the risk of adolescent drug use. *Journal of Primary Prevention*, 26, 529-551.

Bahr, S. J., Marcos, A. C., and Maughan, S. L. (1995). Family, educational and peer influences on the alcohol use of female and male adolescents. *Journal of Studies on Alcohol*, 56, 457-469.

Brown, P. (2002). Smoking increases among teenagers in eastern Europe. *British Medical Journal*, 324, 442.

Chen, C, Greenberger, E., Lester, J., Don, Q., and Guo, M. (1998). A cross-cultural study of peer correlates of adolescent misconduct. *Developmental Psychology*, 34, 770-781.

Chirkov, V-I., and Ryan, R. M. (2001). Parent and teacher autonomy-support in Russian and U.S. adolescents: Common effects on well-being and academic motivation. *Journal of Cross-Cultural Psychology*, 32, 618-635.

Christensen, P. (2004). The health-promoting family: A conceptual framework for future research. *Social Science and Medicine*, 59, 377-387.

Deković, M. (1999). Risk and protective factors in the development of problem behavior during adolescence. *Journal of Youth and Adolescence*, 28, 667-685.

Field, T., Diego, M., and Sanders, C. (2002). Adolescents' parent and peer relationships. *Adolescence*, 37, 121-130.

Fitzpatrick, K. M. (1997a). Aggression and environmental risk among low-income African-American youth. *Journal of Adolescent Health*, 21, 172-178.

Fitzpatrick, K. M. (1997b). Fighting among America's youth: A risk and protective factors approach. *Journal of Health and Social Behavior*, 38, 131-148.

Fitzpatrick, K. M., Piko, B. F., and Wright, D. R. (2005). A tale of two cities: Health-compromising behaviors between Hungarian and American youth. Annals of Sociology of Children. In L. E. Bass (Ed.), *Sociological Studies of Children and Youth* (Vol. 10., pp. 189-212). Amsterdam: Elsevier.

Formoso, D., Gonzales, N. A., and Aiken, L. S. (2000). Family conflict and children's internalizing and externalizing behavior: Protective factors. *American Journal of Community Psychology*, 28, 175-199.

Frey, C. U., and Röthlisberger, C. (1996). Social support in healthy adolescents. *Journal of Youth and Adolescence*, 25, 17-31.

Gilvarry, E. (2000). Substance abuse in young people. *Journal of Child Psychology and Psychiatry*, 41, 55-80.

Gray, M. R., and Steinberg, L. (1999). Unpacking authoritative parenting: reassessing a multidimensional construct. *Journal of Marriage and the Family*, 61, 574-587.

Harland, P., Reijneveld, S. A., Brugman, E., Verloove-Vanhorick, S. P., and Verhulst, F. C. (2002). Family factors and life events as risk factors for behavioural and emotional problems in children. *European Child and Adolescent Psychiatry*, 11, 176-184.

Hawkins, J. D., Catalano, R. F., and Miller, J. Y. (1992). Risk and protective factors for alcohol and other drug problems in adolescence and early adulthood: Implications for substance abuse prevention. *Psychological Bulletin*, 112, 64-105.

Jackson, C., Henriksen, L., and Foshee, V. A. (1998). The Authoritative Parenting Index: Predicting health risk behaviors among children and adolescents. *Health Education and Behavior*, 25(3), 319-337.

Jaffee, S. R., Moffitt, T. E., Caspi, A., Taylor, A., and Arseneault, L. (2002). Influence of adult domestic violence on children's internalizing and externalizing problems: an environmentally informative twin study. *Journal of the American Academy of Child and Adolescent Psychiatry*, 41, 1095-1103.

Li, X., Feigelman, S., and Stanton, B. (2000). Perceived parental monitoring and health risk behaviors among urban low-income African-American children and adolescents. *Journal of Adolescent Health*, 27, 43-48.

Li, X., Stanton, B., and Feigelman, S. (2000). Impact of perceived parental monitoring on adolescent risk behavior over 4 years. *Journal of Adolescent Health*, 27, 49-56.

Norton, D. E., Sivarajan-Froelicher, E., Waters, C. M., and Carrieri-Kohlman, V. (2003). Parental influence on models of primary prevention of cardiovascular disease on children. *European Journal of Cardiovascular Nursing, 2*, 311-322.

Paterson, J., Pryor, J., and Field, J. (1995). Adolescent attachment and friends in relation to aspects of self-esteem. *Journal of Youth and Adolescents*, 24, 365-376.

Piko B. (2000). Perceived social support from parents and peers: which is the stronger predictor of adolescent substance use? *Substance Use and Misuse*, 35, 617-630.

Piko B. (2001). Smoking in adolescence: Do attitudes matter? *Addictive Behaviors*, 26, 201-217.

Piko B., and Fitzpatrick K. (2001). Health risk behaviors in adolescence: Comparison of Hungarian and American youth. *Health Education*, 42, 249-252. (in Hungarian)

Piko B. F, Fitzpatrick, K. M., and Wright, D. R. (2005). A risk and protective factors framework for understanding youth's externalizing problem behavior in two different cultural settings. *European Child and Adolescent Psychiatry*, 14, 95-103.

Piko B., Luszczynska, A. Gibbons, F. X., and Teközel, M. (2005). A culture-based study of personal and social influences of adolescent smoking. *European Journal of Public Health*, 15, 393-398.

Poikolainen, K. (2002). Antecedens of substance use in adolescence. *Current Opinion in Psychiatry*, 15, 241-245.

Radziszewska, B., Richardson, J. L., Dent, C. W., and Flay, B. R. (1996). Parenting style and adolescent depressive symptoms, smoking, and academic achievement: Ethnic,   gender, and SES differences. *Journal of Behavioral Medicine*, 19, 289-305.

Rohner, R. P., and Britner, P. A. (2002). Worldwide mental health correlates of parental acceptance – rejection: Review of cross-cultural evidence. *Cross-Cultural Research*, 36, 16-47.

Sargent, J. D., and Dalton, M. (2001). Does parental disapproval of smoking prevent adolescents from becoming established smokers? *Pediatrics*, 108, 1256-1262.

Search Institute (1998). *Search Institute Profiles of Student Life Administration Manual*. Search Institute, Minneapolis, MN.

Simons-Morton, B., Haynie, D. L., Crump, A. D., Eitel, P., and Saylor, K. E. (2001). Peer and parent influences on smoking and drinking among early adolescents. *Health Education and Behavior*, 28, 95-107.

Steinberg, L., Fletcher, A., and Darling, N. (1994). Parental monitoring and peer influences on adolescent substance use. *Pediatrics*, 93, 1060-1064.

Steptoe, A., and Wardle, J. (1992). Cognitive predictors of health behavior in contrasting regions of Europe. *British Journal of Clinical Psychology*, 31, 485-502.

Stronski, S. M., Ireland, M., Michaud, P.-A., Narring, F., and Resnick, M. D. (2000). Protective correlates of stages in adolescent substance use: A Swiss National Study. *Journal of Adolescent Health*, 26, 420-427.

Vazsonyi, A. T. (2003). Parent-adolescent relations and problem behaviors: Hungary, the Netherlands, Switzerland, and the United States. *Marriage and Family Review,* 35, 161-187.

Wood, M. D., Read, J. P., Mitchell, R. E., and Brand, N. H. (2004). Do parents still matter? Parent and peer influences on alcohol involvement among recent high school graduates. *Psychology of Addictive Behaviors*, 18, 19-30.

In: Substance Abuse among Adolescents ISBN: 978-1-61122-933-2
Editor: Isabelle M. Giordano © 2011 Nova Science Publishers, Inc.

Chapter 3

FLUOXETINE TRIAL FOR THE CANNABIS-RELATED SYMPTOMS OF COMORBID ADOLESCENTS

Jack R. Cornelius*, Oscar G. Bukstein,
Duncan B. Clark, James K. Matta, Ihsan M. Salloum
and D. Scott Wood
Department of Psychiatry, Western Psychiatric Institute and Clinic,
University of Pittsburgh School of Medicine, USA

ABSTRACT

We conducted a first open-label acute phase and long-term (5-year) follow-up study of fluoxetine in 13 adolescents with comorbid major depression and an alcohol use disorder, twelve of whom also had a lifetime history of having used cannabis. Cannabis-related symptoms were assessed using the DSM-IV diagnostic criteria for cannabis

---

* Address correspondence to Dr. Cornelius, University of Pittsburgh School of Medicine, 3811 O'Hara Street, PAARC Suite, Pittsburgh, PA 15213. Presented at the 2006 American Society on Addiction Medicine (ASAM) Annual Meeting, May 4-7, 2006; at the 2006 American Psychiatric Association (APA) Annual Meeting, May 20-25, 2006; at the Annual Meeting of the College on Problems of Drug Dependence (CPDD), June 17-22, 2006; and at the 2006 Annual Meeting of the Research Society on Alcoholism (RSA), June 23-29, 2006. E-mail: jcornel@pitt.edu.

dependence. During the acute phase study, the number of DSM-IV diagnostic criteria for cannabis dependence significantly decreased among the ten subjects who exhibited any of those cannabis dependence symptoms at baseline. In addition, the number of subjects who met full DSM-IV diagnostic criteria (at least three criteria items) for cannabis dependence decreased from five to zero, which was a significant decrease. The medication was very well tolerated during the treatment trial. No subjects demonstrated current cannabis dependence at the 5-year follow-up evaluation. Based on the promising findings of this pilot study, the authors of this study were recently funded by the National Institute on Drug Abuse (NIDA) to conduct a double-blind, placebo-controlled trial of fluoxetine in adolescent patients with major depression and a comorbid cannabis use disorder (R01 DA019142). However, the results of that double-blind placebo-controlled study will not be known for five years.

Keywords: Cannabis use disorder; Fluoxetine; Adolescents; Major depression.

INTRODUCTION

Cannabis is the most commonly used illicit substance in the United States, and has been so for decades.[1-3] The vast majority of individuals who use cannabis or who have a cannabis use disorder (CUD) are young, being in their teens or twenties.[3] Comorbidity is the rule rather than the exception among young people with substance use disorders, including those with cannabis use disorders.[4] Depressive disorders are one of the most common comorbid diagnoses in clinical populations of adolescents with substance use disorders.[5] Major depressive disorder (MDD) is strongly related to cannabis abuse and dependence, as shown by the fact that patients with a cannabis use disorder are 4.5 times more likely to demonstrate major depression than those without a cannabis use disorder.[6] Despite the prevalence of this comorbid condition (CUD/MDD) among adolescents, there have been no randomized clinical trials of pharmacological interventions among cannabis-dependent individuals, including those with or without comorbid major depression.[7-9] Consequently, to date, no medication has been shown to alter cannabis self-administration by humans.[9] Also, because of lack of studies, it is currently unclear whether antidepressant medications such as fluoxetine demonstrate efficacy for decreasing the depressive symptoms and/or the cannabis-related symptoms of adolescents with comorbid major depression and a cannabis use disorder.

The study described in this report is a first open-label acute phase and long-term (five-year) follow-up study of fluoxetine in adolescents with comorbid major depression and an alcohol use disorder, twelve of whom had also used cannabis during their lifetime. The alcohol and depression-related findings from this study have already been described elsewhere,[10] though the cannabis-related findings have not been the focus of our previous publications. The purpose of this study was to conduct a preliminary assessment of the efficacy of fluoxetine for decreasing the cannabis-related symptoms of comorbid adolescents. Cannabis-related symptoms were assessed using the DSM-IV diagnostic criteria for cannabis dependence. We hypothesized that the number of DSM-IV criteria for cannabis dependence would significantly decrease during the 12-week acute phase study, and that these symptoms would continue to show a significant decrease compared to baseline levels when assessed at the five-year follow-up assessment. We also hypothesized that the number of subjects demonstrating full criteria (at least three of the DSM criteria) for cannabis dependence would significantly decrease during the acute phase of the study, and would continue to still be significantly lower at the five-year follow-up evaluation.

METHODS

Subjects

All patients were recruited from radio and newspaper advertisements. Before entry into the protocol, the study was explained, and written informed consent was obtained after all procedures had been fully explained. The study was approved by the University of Pittsburgh Institutional Review Board.

Thirteen patients participated in the 12-week acute phase of the study, including 3 males and 10 females. Twelve of those thirteen individuals reported a lifetime history of cannabis use. Twelve of these subjects were Caucasian American, and one was African American. The mean age was 18.8 years (S.D.=1.4 years, range=15-19) . Inclusion criteria for the acute phase included the following: 1) current DSM-IV diagnoses of major depression and either alcohol dependence or alcohol abuse at baseline, following any needed detoxification and a subsequent 1-week wash-out period; 2) consuming at least 10 drinks in the month prior to entering the study; and 3) a score of greater than 12 at baseline on the 24-item Hamilton Depression Rating Scale; and 4) age between 15 and 19 years. No one who participated in the acute phase study was excluded from participation in the five-year follow-up study. Potential subjects were excluded for most substance dependence diagnoses, such as diagnoses of opiate dependence, cocaine dependence, or sedative/hypnotic dependence, but cannabis dependence and nicotine dependence did not serve as exclusionary diagnoses. Ten of the 13 subjects reported that they were currently using cannabis at the baseline of the acute phase study. In addition, 10 of the 13 subjects subsequently used cannabis at some time during the 12-week acute phase study. Substance abuse did not serve as an exclusionary criterion.

Procedures

Subjects were treated using an open-label study design. All subjects were initially given one 10-mg capsule of fluoxetine each morning for the first two weeks. The medication dose was increased to 20 mg of fluoxetine each morning thereafter if they had not demonstrated any medication side effects on the 10-mg dose. No subjects demonstrated any medication side effects on the 10-mg dose, so all subjects were increased to the 20-mg dose. All subjects also received manualized psychotherapy. That psychotherapy consisted of supportive therapy, in combination with cognitive behavioral and motivational enhancement therapy. Appointments were conducted every week for the first four weeks of the study, and were conducted every other week for the remaining 8 weeks of the study. During each appointment the subjects' symptoms were rated, and the subjects participated in a psychotherapy session with a counselor and a medication check session with a physician.[11]

Substance use disorder diagnoses and major depressive disorder were assessed at baseline, at the conclusion of the 12-week acute phase study, and at the follow-up evaluations using the Substance Use Disorders Section of the Structured Clinical Interview for the DSM (SCID) and the Schedule for Affective Disorders and Schizophrenia for School Age Children (K-SADS), respectively. Cannabis-related symptoms were assessed using the DSM-IV diagnostic criteria for cannabis dependence, as noted on the SCID.[12] Observer-rated depressive symptoms were assessed with the 24-item Hamilton Rating Scale for Depression. Self-rated depressive symptoms were assessed using the Beck Depression Inventory. All ratings for the study were performed by an experienced rater who had demonstrated inter-rater reliability on all major measures. All 13 subjects completed all of the weekly rating sessions during the acute phase of the study.

A total of 10 of the 13 patients who had participated in the acute phase study signed informed consent to participate in a long-term (5-year) follow-up. All 10 of those subjects who had signed informed consent for the follow-up study subsequently completed the follow-up assessments. Nine of those ten subjects had used cannabis during their lifetime, and five of the ten had a current diagnosis of cannabis dependence. Following completion of the 12-week acute phase medication trial, the subjects were referred back to their local doctors for long-term naturalistic treatment provided by physicians and therapists unrelated to the study. The subjects did not receive protocol medications during the follow-up period, but instead received evaluation and treatment as determined by their local treating physician. Most former subjects (n=6) had used an Selective Serotonin Reuptake Inhibitor (SSRI) antidepressant during the course of the follow-up phase. Additional details about the methods of the long-term follow-up study are published elsewhere.[10]

Statistical analyses were performed using paired *t* tests for continuous measures and using chi-square tests for categorical measures. All tests were two-tailed. Outcome measures were calculated using intention-to-treat analyses.

RESULTS

During the acute phase study, the number of DSM-IV diagnostic criteria for cannabis dependence significantly decreased among the ten subjects who exhibited any of those cannabis dependence symptoms at baseline (mean decrease=2.1, df=9, t=2.69, p=0.025). In addition, during the course of the acute phase of treatment, the number of subjects who met full DSM-IV diagnostic criteria (at least three criteria items were present) for cannabis dependence decreased from five to zero, which was a significant decrease (Pearson Chi-Square=6.96, df=1, p=0.008). Fluoxetine was very well tolerated by the individuals participating in this study. No subjects reported significant side effects from fluoxetine.

At the five-year follow-up evaluation, there were no subjects with cannabis dependence, which was significantly fewer than had been noted at baseline (Person Chi-Square=6.96, df=1, p=0.008). Similarly, the number of DSM IV diagnostic criteria for Cannabis Dependence at the five-year follow-up evaluation was significantly fewer than had been demonstrated at baseline (t=2.52, df=9, p=0.033).

As previously reported, the acute phase (12-week) results from the study also demonstrated a significant within-group reduction of number of DSM-IV MDD criteria and number of DSM-IV alcohol dependence criteria among our adolescent comorbid population, and these reductions persisted at the five-year follow-up evaluation.[10]

DISCUSSION

This study provides preliminary data from what we believe is a first acute phase and five-year naturalistic follow-up study evaluating the efficacy of a SSRI antidepressant medication plus psychotherapy in the treatment of adolescents with a trimorbid condition involving a cannabis use disorder in addition to major depressive disorder and an alcohol use disorder. The results of this study suggest efficacy for fluoxetine plus psychotherapy in decreasing the DSM-IV diagnostic symptoms (criteria) of cannabis dependence. However, it is unclear to what extent that fluoxetine was responsible for this clinical improvement in cannabis-related symptoms versus the extent that improvement resulted from psychotherapy or developmental changes, since the study was an open label study. These results are consistent with the results of a secondary analysis involving a double-blind, placebo-controlled study of fluoxetine in trimorbid adults with a cannabis use disorder in addition to major depression and an alcohol use disorder, which suggested efficacy for fluoxetine in decreasing the cannabis use of that adult trimorbid population.[13-14]

Our current study is limited by its modest sample size, the lack of a control group, and the naturalistic nature of its study design during the long-term follow-up assessments. The findings of our current study suggest that double-blind, placebo-controlled studies are warranted to assess the safety and efficacy of SSRI antidepressants in adolescents and young adults with comorbid major depression and a cannabis use disorder. Prospective, longitudinal long-term follow-up studies are also warranted to clarify the long-term efficacy of SSRI antidepressants and other medications among comorbid adolescents, and to clarify the long-term course of various subgroups within that population.[15-16] Based on the promising findings of this pilot study, the authors of this paper were recently funded by the National Institute on Drug Abuse (NIDA) to conduct a double-blind, placebo-controlled study to assess the efficacy of fluoxetine (20 mg) for the treatment of adolescents with comorbid major depression and a cannabis use disorder (R01 DA019142). The results of that double-blind, placebo-controlled study will not be known for five years.

AUTHOR'S NOTES

This research was supported in part by grants from the National Institute on Drug Abuse (R01 DA019142, R01 DA14635, R01 DA019992, and P50 DA05605); from the National Institute on Alcohol Abuse and Alcoholism (R01 AA013370, R01 AA015173, R01 AA11292, K02 AA00291, and K24 AA15320); and a grant from the Veterans Administration (MIRECC to VISN 4).

REFERENCES

[1]   Anthony JC, Warner LA, Kessler RC. Comparative epidemiology of dependence on tobacco, alcohol, controlled substances, and inhalants: basic findings from the National Comorbidity Survey. *Exp. Clin. Psychopharmacol.* 1994; 2:244-268.

[2]   Dennis M, Babor TF, Roebuck MC, Donaldson J. Changing the focus: the case for recognizing and treating cannabis use disorders. *Addiction.* 2002: 97 (Suppl 1):4-15.

[3]   Compton WM, Grant BF, Colliver JD, Glantz MD, Stinson FS. Prevalence of marijuana use disorders in the United States, 1991-1992 and 2001-2002. *JAMA.* 2004; 291:2114-2121.

[4]   Kessler RC, Walters EE. Epidemiology of DSM-III-R major depression and minor depression among adolescents and young adults in the *National Comorbidity Survey. Depr. and Anx.* 1998; 7:3-14.

[5]   Bukstein OG, Glancy LJ, Kaminer Y. Patterns of affective comorbidity in a clinical population of dually diagnosed adolescent substance abusers. *J. Am. Acad. Child Adol. Psychiatry.* 1992; 31:1041-1045.

[6]   Grant BF. Comorbidity between DSM-IV drug use disorders and major depression: results of a national survey of adults. *J. Subst. Abuse.*1995; 7:481-497.

[7]   McRae AL, Budney AJ, Brady KT. Treatment of marijuana dependence: a review of the literature. *J. Subst. Abuse Treat.* 2003; 24:369-376.

[8]   Copeland J. Developments in the treatment of cannabis use disorder. *Curr. Opinion Psychiatry.* 2004; 17:161-168.

[9]   Hart CL. Increasing treatment options for cannabis dependence: A review of potential pharmacotherapies. *Drug Alcohol. Depend.* 2005; 80:147-150.

[10]   Cornelius JR, Clark DB, Bukstein OG, Birmaher B, Kelly TM, Salloum IM, Walters M, Matta J, Wood DS. Fluoxetine in adolescents with comorbid major depression and an alcohol use disorder: A five-year follow-up study. *J. Dual Disorders.* 2006; 2:9-23.

[11]   Cornelius JR, Bukstein OG, Birmaher B, Salloum IM, Lynch K, Pollock NK, Gershon S, Clark D. Fluoxetine in adolescents with major depression and an alcohol use disorder: An open-label trial. *Addict. Beh.* 2001; 26:735-739.

[12]   Martin CS, Pollock NK, Bukstein BG, Lynch KG. Inter-rater reliability of the SCID alcohol and substance use disorders section among adolescents. *Drug Alcohol. Depend.* 2000; 59:173-176.

[13]   Cornelius JR, Salloum IM, Ehler JG, Jarrett PJ, Cornelius MD, Perel JM, Thase ME, Black A. Fluoxetine in depressed alcoholics: a double-blind, placebo-controlled trial. *Arch. Gen. Psychiatry.* 1997; 54:700-705.

[14]   Cornelius JR, Salloum IM, Haskett RF, Ehler JG, Jarrett PJ, Thase ME, Perel JM. Fluoxetine vs. placebo for the marijuana use of depressed alcoholics. *Addict. Behav.* 1999; 24:111-114.

[15]   Chung T, Maisto SA, Cornelius JR, Martin CS. Adolescents' alcohol and drug use trajectories in the year following treatment. *J. Stud. Alcohol.* 2004; 65:105-114.

[16]   Cornelius JR, Maisto SA, Martin CS, Bukstein OG, Salloum IM, Daley DC, Wood DS, Clark DB. Major depression associated with earlier relapse in treated teens with AUD. *Addict. Beh.* 2004; 29:979-982.

In: Substance Abuse among Adolescents   ISBN: 978-1-61122-933-2
Editor: Isabelle M. Giordano   © 2011 Nova Science Publishers, Inc.

Chapter 4

WAR ON DRUGS: THE NATIONAL YOUTH ANTI-DRUG MEDIA CAMPAIGN

Mark Eddy

ABSTRACT

Authorization of the National Youth Anti-Drug Media Campaign, a multi-media federal program to persuade America's youth not to use drugs, expired at the end of FY2002. H.R. 2829 (passed by the House on March 13, 2006) and S. 2560 (reported by the Senate Judiciary Committee on May 25, 2006) would reauthorize the media campaign, along with the other programs run by the Office of National Drug Control Policy (ONDCP). H.R. 5576, the House-passed appropriations bill that funds ONDCP, proposes $100 million for the campaign for FY2007. The media campaign's effectiveness has been questioned, and the program has engendered its share of controversy. Nevertheless, ONDCP, the office of the "drug czar," is optimistic that recent changes in campaign strategy will help to reduce illegal drug use by young people. This report will be updated as legislative activity occurs.

BACKGROUND

Although it accounts for less than 1% of the federal drug-control budget, the National Youth Anti-Drug Media Campaign is, for many Americans, the most visible aspect of the war on drugs. This is by design. The campaign's strategy is based on the belief that its efforts to persuade young people not to use illegal drugs will be effective only if its messages are seen repeatedly by large numbers of youth and by the adults who influence them — such as parents, teachers, clergy, and mentors. According to congressional testimony in 2003, the campaign's broadcast, print, and Internet ads reach about 90% of all teens at least four times per week at a cost to taxpayers of less than $8 per teenager per year [1].

The media campaign was authorized by the Drug-Free Media Campaign Act of 1998 [2]. This law, less than two pages in length, instructed the Director of the Office of National Drug Control Policy (commonly referred to as the "Drug Czar") to "conduct a national media campaign ... for the purpose of reducing and preventing drug abuse among young people in the United States." The antidrug media campaign is an attempt at behavior change, forms of which have been used in other government campaigns and are used by nongovernmental organizations and commercial marketers. It seeks to reinforce existing antidrug attitudes in youth and adults and reverse the attitudes of those who have positive ideas about illegal drugs, thereby reducing the number of young Americans who use illegal drugs.

The media campaign is a public-private partnership. Most of the campaign's advertisements have been produced by the Partnership for a Drug Free America (PDFA), a nonprofit organization that recruits advertising agencies to develop creative concepts on a pro bono basis. Appropriated media campaign funds are then used to cover the costs of actually making the antidrug ads. The Partnership itself receives minimal federal funding. Its relationship with the Office of National Drug Control Policy (ONDCP) has made PDFA the single largest public service initiative in the history of advertising.

In addition to media ads, the campaign has a non-advertising component consisting of public outreach and specialized supporting communications efforts. These include the operation of antidrug websites, meetings with news and entertainment writers and editors to encourage them to promote antidrug messages, and a corporate sponsorship program under which leading corporations insert antidrug messages into their own communications with their customers and the public.

PROGRAM FUNDING

The Drug-Free Media Campaign Act authorized appropriations to ONDCP of $195 million for each fiscal year from 1999 through 2002 — a total of $975 million — to run the campaign. The Administration had originally proposed a somewhat less generous $175 million per year budget — for a total of $875 million — although subsequent budget requests were for larger amounts. Actual appropriations through FY2002 of $930 million amounted to $55 million more than originally proposed and $45 million less than the authorized level.

Although the authorization expired at the end of FY2002, the Administration has continued to request funding for the campaign, and Congress has continued to provide appropriations at levels less than requested in the President's annual budget request and less than appropriated in previous years (see Table 1). Congress has reduced funding for the media campaign every year since FY2001, from $185 million in that year's budget to $100 million in FY2006, an overall cut of 47%. Nevertheless, over the nine years of the campaign's existence, Congress has appropriated nearly $1.5 billion to the media campaign.

The President's budget submission for FY2004 provided the following comment about the campaign (*Appendix*, p. 1053):

> In 2002, the Office of Management and Budget (OMB) conducted a systematic review of more than 200 Federal programs to assess their performance in a number of areas. The National Youth Anti-Drug Media Campaign has not demonstrated the results sought and does not yet have adequate performance measures and related goals. The OMB recommended actions include (1) continued emphasis on developing acceptable performance measures and goals; (2) allowing sufficient time for the effects of recent ONDCP actions to be realized before pursuing changes to the program; (3) seeking no funding increases for the program; and (4) making FY2005 funding contingent upon improved results.

Congressional skepticism about the program persists, as evidenced by declining levels of funding for the campaign.

Table 1. Media Campaign Appropriations, by Fiscal Year
(dollars in millions)

Fiscal Year	Authorized	Administration Request	House Passed	Senate Passed	Final Appropriation
1998	$195.0	$175.0	$195.0	$110.0	$195.0
1999	195.0	195.0	185.0	110.0	185.0
2000	195.0	185.0	195.0	96.5	185.0
2001	195.0	185.0	185.0	98.7	185.0
2002	195.0	185.0	180.0	185.0	180.0
2003	—	180.0	170.0	100.0	150.0
2004	—	170.0	150.0	100.0	145.0
2005	—	145.0	120.0	100.0	120.0
2006	—	120.0	120.0	95.0	100.0
2007	—	120.0	100.0	TBD	TBD

Source: Table prepared by Congressional Research Service (CRS) from Administration budget requests and from appropriation bills. (Amounts shown are pre-rescission; rescissions were 0.38% in FY2000, 0.22% in FY2001, 0.65% in FY2003, and 0.59% in FY2004).

EARLY IMPLEMENTATION OF THE CAMPAIGN

Phase I of the campaign, January-July 1998, consisted of a 12-city test pilot of ads addressed to various ethnic and geographic audiences. Audience awareness surveys and focus groups were conducted. Phase II, August 1998-July 1999, moved the campaign's testing and evaluation to the national stage with antidrug ads on television, radio, print, and outdoor media. Internet sites for youth, parents, and community partners were launched. Partnerships were begun with corporations, community antidrug coalitions, and state and local governments. Research efforts continued.

In 1999, after conducting a series of panels composed of national experts in public health, social marketing, advertising, and youth behavior change, ONDCP organized Phase III of the campaign. The decision was made to target the campaign's prevention efforts toward youths aged 9 to 18 but with an emphasis on so-called "tweens," those aged 11 to 13 (7th and 8th graders). National surveys showed that drug use first began at the ages of 11 to 13, but was not yet widespread. It was believed that focusing on these younger youth would be the most effective strategy. "Stopping drug use before it starts" became a familiar refrain of then-Drug Czar Barry McCaffrey. Phase III commenced in August 1999 with all elements in place, including additional partnerships with national media, entertainment, and sports organizations as well as civic, professional, and community groups.

THE MATCHING REQUIREMENT AND AN EARLY CONTROVERSY

The campaign's authorizing legislation has a matching requirement. Media companies that are paid by the campaign to run antidrug ads are required to donate an equal amount of advertising time or space or other in-kind contributions to the antidrug effort. ONDCP contracts with the Advertising Council to run this National Media Match Program, which has garnered $447 million worth of pro bono TV and radio time for public service announcements (PSAs). In addition to the campaign's core ads, the matching requirement can be met by airing the PSAs of other agencies or groups — such as the YMCA — whose programs reinforce ONDCP's youth drug prevention strategy.

Early in the program, ONDCP began giving credit toward the matching requirement to television networks whose programs contained antidrug story lines. The networks could then reclaim the credited time it owed to the government and resell it to commercial advertisers at the going rate. Some magazines participating in the campaign also were credited with meeting the matching requirement by printing stories or editorials with antidrug content. Under this scheme, the networks earned $21.8 million in FY1999 by selling airtime that, in the absence of the credits for antidrug messages embedded in their programs, would have been donated to the campaign under the matching requirement [3].

This practice was publicized in January 2000, in the online magazine *Salon*, by freelance reporter Daniel Forbes, who also claimed that, in some cases, ONDCP was reviewing scripts and suggesting changes to make shows conform to the campaign's antidrug message [4]. The next day, the story appeared on the front page of the *Washington Post* [5] and was picked up by other media outlets, resulting in congressional hearings at which ONDCP officials denied influencing the content of TV shows and magazine articles. Following the controversy, FY2001 appropriations language prohibited the practice of crediting media outlets on the basis of story content [6]. At least one law review article has deemed the practice unconstitutional [7].

OVERSIGHT AND EVALUATION

The campaign's authorizing and appropriations language both require rigorous evaluation of the program. ONDCP has allocated more than $50 million for research and evaluation of the program. The National Institute on Drug Abuse (NIDA) manages the Phase III evaluation process for ONDCP and awarded the prime evaluation contract to Westat, Inc. Results are derived from a nationally representative household survey of youths and parents. In May 2002, NIDA released a Westat evaluation report that found little evidence that the youth campaign had had direct, favorable effects between 2000 and 2001 on drug use by young Americans, although it was found to modify parental behavior [8]. In its subsequent November 2002 report, Westat stated:

> There is little evidence of direct favorable Campaign effects on youth. There is no statistically significant decline in marijuana use to date, and some evidence for an increase in use from 2000 to 2001. Nor are there improvements in beliefs and attitudes about marijuana use between 2000 and the first half of 2002. Contrarily, there are some unfavorable trends in youth anti-marijuana beliefs. Also there is no tendency for those reporting more exposure to Campaign messages to hold more desirable beliefs [9].

Congressional appropriators, informed by these and other evaluations of the media campaign, have frequently expressed concern about the campaign. For example, after noting that total appropriations since the inception of the campaign had exceeded $1 billion, the FY2003 appropriations conference report stated: "The conferees are deeply disturbed by the lack of evidence that the National Youth Anti-Drug Media Campaign has had any appreciable impact on youth drug use.... If the campaign continues to fail to demonstrate effectiveness, then the Committees will be compelled to reevaluate the use of taxpayer money to support the Media Campaign" [10].

A controversial series of ads, which began running during the 2002 Super Bowl, painted drug users as implicit supporters of terrorism by indirectly providing money to terrorists. These ads were criticized as misleading and ineffective in media stories. Some critics contended that it is drug prohibition laws — not drug users — that make possible huge, illegal drug profits, some of which might be used to fund acts of terrorism. Moreover, the ads target young, infrequent users who do not account for the vast bulk of drug use — and therefore drug revenues. These ads, which are no longer run, also created friction between ONDCP and PDFA, with PDFA considering the ads off-target.

CHANGES IN STRATEGY

ONDCP Director John P. Walters convened a task force in February 2002 to examine strategic issues affecting campaign performance. The group agreed on significant changes in campaign strategy. Recognizing that the sharpest increase in drug use occurs among youth aged 14 to 16 (9th and 10th graders), the campaign's focus was shifted from "tweens" to these older teens. More rigorous testing of ads was also decided upon. In the past, not all ads were tested before they ran. Now, all TV ads would be thoroughly tested against more demanding standards before being aired. There would also be earlier involvement by ONDCP in the advertising development process.

The release of Westat's May 2002 evaluation resulted in another important change. It was decided that the campaign would concentrate its efforts against marijuana. Walters said in a hearing that "it is clear that we cannot expect to make progress toward our goal of reducing youth drug use until we significantly reduce the use of marijuana, the preponderant drug of choice among youth" [11]. H.R. 2829 (sec. 12(a)) would reinforce this anti-marijuana focus of the campaign with its congressional findings on the harmfulness of the drug and its provision that "the Director [of ONDCP] may emphasize prevention of youth marijuana use" in the advertising and other activities of the media campaign.

Two more changes were revealed by ONDCP Chief of Staff Chris Marston at the House hearing in March 2003 [12]. Previously, 60% of campaign ad expenditures had been directed at adults, 40% at youth. Marston announced a reversal of that ratio. He also said that the campaign would introduce the theme of treatment in its ads, beginning with an emphasis on early intervention, in an attempt to reach youth who use drugs on a regular basis or who are suspected of using drugs. Taken together, according to Marston's testimony, all of these changes "mark a substantially new and essentially re-directed Media Campaign."

REAUTHORIZING LEGISLATION IN THE 109TH CONGRESS

H.R. 2829 and S. 2560, bills to reauthorize ONDCP, would extend the media campaign and authorize appropriations. H.R. 2829, as amended, passed the House on March 13, 2006, and has been sent to the Senate. S. 2560 was reported by the Senate Committee on the Judiciary on May 25, 2006. For analysis on how these bills would affect the media campaign, see CRS Report RL32352, *War on Drugs: Reauthorization of the Office of National Drug Control Policy*, by Mark Eddy.

REFERENCES

[1]   The facts cited in this paper, unless otherwise noted, are drawn from U.S. Congress, House Committee on Government Reform, *ONDCP Reauthorization: The National Youth Anti-Drug Media Campaign*, 108th Cong., 1st sess., Mar. 27, 2003 (Washington: GPO, 2003).

[2]   P.L. 105-277, Division D, Title I, Sect. 102, Oct. 21, 1998; 112 Stat. 2681-752; 21 U.S.C. 1801.

[3]   U.S. Congress, House, Committee on Commerce, Subcommittee on Telecommunications, Trade, and Consumer Protection, *The White House, the Networks and TV Censorship*, hearing, 106th Cong., 2nd sess., Feb. 9, 2000 (Washington: GPO, 2000), p. 40.

[4]   Daniel Forbes, "Prime-Time Propaganda," *Salon*, Jan. 13, 2000. Forbes' stories on this issue can be accessed in the archives of Salon.com.

[5]   Howard Kurtz and Sharon Waxman, "White House Cut Anti-Drug Deal with TV," *Washington Post*, Jan. 14, 2000, p. A1.

[6]   U.S. Congress, Conference Committees, 2000, *Making Omnibus Consolidated and Emergency Supplemental Appropriations for Fiscal Year 2001*, conference report to accompany H.R. 4577, H.Rept. 106-1033, 106th Cong., 2nd sess. (Washington: GPO, 2000), pp. 390-391.

[7] Ariel Berschadsky, "White House Anti-Drug Policy: Statutory and Constitutional Implications," *Cardozo Arts and Entertainment Law Journal*, vol. 19, 2001, p. 199.

[8] Vanessa O'Connell, "Drug Czar Says Ad Campaign Has Flopped," *Wall Street Journal*, May 14, 2002, p. B1.

[9] Robert Hornik, et al., *Evaluation of the National Youth Anti-Drug Media Campaign: Fifth Semi-Annual Report of Findings Executive Summary* (Rockville, MD: Westat, Nov. 2002), p. xi.

[10] U.S. Congress, Conference Committees, 2003, *Making Further Continuing Appropriations for the Fiscal Year 2003, and for Other Purposes*, conference report to accompany H.J.Res. 2, H.Rept. 108-10, 108th Cong., 1st sess. (Washington: GPO, 2003), pp. 1345-1346.

[11] U.S. Congress, Senate Committee on Appropriations, Subcommittee on Treasury and General Government, *Effectiveness of the National Youth Anti-Drug Media Campaign*, special hearing, 107th Cong., 2nd sess., June 19, 2002 (Washington: GPO, 2002), p. 14. Actually, alcohol, followed by tobacco, is the most prevalent drug used by America's youth, and such drug use, while legal for adults, is not legal for youth.

[12] U.S. Congress, House Committee on Government Reform, *ONDCP Reauthorization: The National Youth Anti-Drug Media Campaign*, 108th Cong., 1st sess., Mar. 27, 2003 (Washington: GPO, 2003).

In: Substance Abuse among Adolescents   ISBN: 978-1-61122-933-2
Editor: Isabelle M. Giordano   © 2011 Nova Science Publishers, Inc.

Chapter 5

COCAINE-DEPENDENT PATIENTS WITH ANTISOCIAL PERSONALITY DISORDER

Nena Messina[1], David Farabee and Richard Rawson
UCLA Integrated Substance Abuse Programs, USA

ABSTRACT

This study compared the efficacy of two commonly used treatment approaches (cognitive–behavioral treatment and contingency manage-ment) for the treatment of cocaine dependence among methadone-maintained patients with and without antisocial personality disorder (ASPD). This disorder is strongly associated with substance abuse and recent study findings provide a strong argument against the perception that substance abusers with ASPD are unresponsive to drug treatment.

Method: Patients were randomly assigned to four study conditions including cognitive–behavioral treatment (CBT), contingency manage-ment (CM), CBT with CM, or methadone maintenance (also the control

---

[1] Corresponding Author: Nena Messina, Ph.D., 1640 S. Sepulveda Blvd., Suite 200 Los Angeles, CA. 90025, Phone: (310) 445-0874 ext. 335, Fax: (310) 312-0559, nmessina@ucla.edu, dfarabee@ucla.edu, matrixex@ucla.edu

condition). The Structural Clinical Interview for Mental Disorders–IV was administered to 108 patients to assess ASPD.

Hypotheses: We hypothesized that ASPD patients in the three treatment conditions (CBT, CM, CBT + CM) would have better treatment responsivity over the 16-week course of treatment than would ASPD patients in the control condition (MM). Moreover, we hypothesized that there would be a cumulative treatment effect among ASPD patients over the course of treatment, with good performance in the CBT condition, better performance in the CM condition, and optimum performance in the CBT + CM condition. Conversely, we hypothesized that the positive treatment effect of CM would decline for the ASPD patients once the incentive was removed (i.e., during the post-treatment outcome period).

Results: A two-way analysis of variance showed that patients with ASPD were more likely to abstain from cocaine use during treatment than patients without ASPD. The strong treatment effect for ASPD patients was primarily due to the CM condition. A series of regression analyses showed that ASPD remained significantly related to CM treatment responsivity while controlling for other related factors.

Conclusion: Monetary incentives appear to reduce cocaine use among substance abusers with ASPD more than among those without ASPD. The results of the present study and other recent publications suggest that substance abusers with ASPD may be more responsive to treatment than previously believed.

INTRODUCTION

Antisocial personality disorder (ASPD) is a personality disorder officially recognized by the American Psychiatric Association and often associated with substance abuse and criminal behavior. The key features of the disorder are outlined in the *Diagnostic and Statistical Manual of Mental Disorders,* fourth edition, commonly known as the DSM-IV. The essential feature of this disorder is "a pervasive pattern of disregard for, and violation of, the rights of others that begins in childhood or early adolescence and continues into adulthood" (American Psychiatric Association, 1994: 645). Common signs of childhood development of ASPD are lying, stealing, fighting, resisting authority, and cruelty to animals. Aggressive sexual behavior, drinking and drug abuse are common in adolescence. Adult manifestations include illegal behavior, deceitfulness, recklessness, violence, job troubles, and marital difficulties. (For a complete description of ASPD, see Messina, 2002.)

Previous research indicates that this disorder is also strongly associated with excessive substance abuse in adulthood, with about 40% to 50% of substance abusers meeting the criteria for ASPD (Messina, Wish, & Nemes, 1999; Tims, DeLeon, & Jainchill, 1994) and approximately 90% of persons diagnosed with ASPD being substance abusers (Gerstley, Alterman, McLellan, & Woody, 1990). In light of the prevalence of ASPD among substance-abusing populations, it became imperative that effective treatment strategies be identified. Thus, the recurring association among ASPD, substance abuse, and crime led to a variety of treatment outcome evaluations for substance abusers with this disorder. Yet, there is a widely held belief among treatment providers that persons with ASPD will not respond well to treatment as a direct result of the symptoms of their disorder (e.g., habitual lying and lack of emotional insight). In fact, treatment providers and therapists alike often state that patients with ASPD will manipulate their therapy for their own self-serving needs (Abram, 1989; Davidson & Neale, 1990; Evans & Sullivan, 1990; Forrest, 1992). As one expert notes: "If it is to their advantage to act cured, they will do so, but they will return to former patterns of behavior at the first opportunity" (Coon, 1983: 465). This belief was substantiated by a frequently cited report that stated that, compared to other types of patients, antisocial opioid abusers responded poorly to both routine drug abuse counseling and specialized psychotherapy (Woody, McLellan, Luborsky, & O'Brien, 1985).

Results from more recent studies that have empirically assessed the relationship between ASPD and substance abuse treatment outcomes have not supported the previous findings regarding this disorder and treatment response (Brooner, Kidorf, King, & Stoller, 1998; Gil, Nolimal, & Crowley, 1992; Messina et al., 1999; Silverman et al., 1998). Gil et al. (1992) compared the treatment outcomes of 55 consecutively admitted methadone maintenance patients with ASPD (42%) and those without ASPD. Although the findings were limited by the small sample and ambiguous design, no significant differences were found between those with and those without ASPD on any 12-month outcome variable (e.g., treatment retention, urine test results, therapy session attendance). It appeared that ASPD patients did as well as those without ASPD in a traditional methadone maintenance program. However, a lack of difference did not necessarily imply good treatment responsivity. The authors reported low overall retention in this sample of clients.

Valliant (1975) had previously speculated that structured behavioral programs with incentives for participation might produce the best results for antisocial opioid patients. Evans and Sullivan (1990) also stated that "[it] is highly unlikely that antisocials will develop genuine remorse and altruistic reasons for staying clean and sober. However, they may be interested if it will help them win at poker, make more money, or stay out of jail" (p. 104).

Brooner and his colleagues (1998) directly tested Valliant's hypothesis regarding the use of incentives. Forty opioid abusers with co-occurring ASPD were randomly assigned to an experimental treatment condition combining methadone maintenance and contingency management techniques (i.e., a structural behavioral intervention using rapid delivery of positive and negative contingencies) or a control condition (i.e., standard methadone maintenance). In the experimental condition, take-home methadone doses and dose alterations were contingent on drug-free urine specimens and counseling session attendance. Preliminary findings did not reveal significant differences between the groups; yet, both groups showed marked reductions in heroin and cocaine use during the 17-week outcome evaluation. The authors contend that these findings are not only contrary to what is commonly thought about ASPD clients in traditional methadone treatment, but also about ASPD clients in enhanced methadone (i.e., methadone maintenance combined with contingency management) treatment programs as well. However, this study was limited by a small sample and by the absence of a non-ASPD control group.

Other contingency management approaches include giving vouchers that are exchangeable for goods and services in response to drug-free urine specimens. Silverman et al. (1998) compared the treatment responsiveness of 59 methadone maintenance patients with ASPD (19%) and without ASPD who were participating in voucher-based cocaine abstinence reinforcement therapy. Patients were randomly assigned to two levels of voucher-based interventions or a control group in which vouchers were given on a noncontingent basis. The authors found that both contingent interventions significantly increased abstinence from cocaine and opiates, compared with the control group. Moreover, a diagnosis of ASPD was unrelated to treatment outcomes. However, the small sample size (and low prevalence of ASPD) may have rendered any differences in outcomes between substance abusers with ASPD and those without ASPD difficult to detect.

Another study explored the relationship of ASPD and treatment outcomes in therapeutic
communities (TCs) with random assignment of (primarily cocaine dependent) respondents to two residential programs differing primarily in length (Messina et al., 1999). TCs often rely on cognitive behavioral methods to change existing behavior patterns. Clients diagnosed as having ASPD (n=166) were

compared to 172 clients with no ASPD on three outcome measures. After controlling for relevant factors, clients with ASPD were as likely to complete treatment as other clients and they exhibited the same patterns of reduced drug use and criminal activity as did non-ASPD clients.

The findings from the above recent studies could indicate that ASPD is not a strong predictor of treatment nonresponsivity, as previously believed. The implications of these findings are important in light of the fact that substance abusers with ASPD are more likely than those without ASPD to engage in violent and serious criminal behaviors (Abram, 1989; Brooner, Schmidt, Felch, & Bigelow, 1992). However, the empirical literature assessing the relationship between ASPD and substance abuse treatment outcomes is lacking, and the existing research is limited by small sample sizes, nonrandom designs, and/or the absence of an appropriate control group. The present study sought to examine the relationship between ASPD and substance abuse treatment responsivity by addressing these primary weaknesses of the literature.

This study directly compares the efficacy of two commonly used treatment approaches (cognitive behavioral treatment and contingency management) for the treatment of cocaine dependence among methadone-maintained patients *with and without* ASPD. These two treatment approaches represent two of the most promising psychological-behavioral approaches for the treatment of substance abuse. However, the rationales for these two approaches differ considerably. Cognitive behavioral treatment (CBT) strategies are based upon social learning principles (Bandura, 1977). These techniques include a wide range of treatment strategies designed to prevent relapse to drug use. The primary focus of CBT is maintaining a habit-changing process. This process is twofold: to prevent the occurrence of initial lapses to drug use after one has embarked on a program of habit change, and to prevent any lapse from escalating into total relapse (Marlatt & Gordon, 1985).

Contingency management (CM) techniques, on the other hand, are founded on principles of operant conditioning (Skinner, 1938). The CM techniques create systems of incentives and disincentives to motivate behavior change. Some positive incentive strategies include take-home methadone doses and cash incentives for drug-free urine specimens. One of the most promising applications of CBT and CM is in the area of cocaine abuse treatment. Cocaine abuse continues to be a serious public health problem and is an important factor in drug-related crime and violence (Everingham & Rydell, 1994). Moreover, cocaine abuse among methadone-maintained patients continues to be a serious challenge for treatment clinicians (Farabee,

Rawson, & McCann, 2002; Rawson, Obert, McCann, & Ling, 1991; Silverman, Chutuape, Bigelow, & Stitzer, 1999). Both CBT and CM have been shown to be effective in treating cocaine-dependent patients (Carroll, 1999; Carroll et al., 1994; Farabee et al., 2002; Foote et al., 1994; Marlatt & Gordon, 1985; Silverman et al., 1996; Silverman et al., 1998; Silverman et al., 1999).

This study offers an excellent opportunity to compare the relative efficacy of an information-based "talk therapy" (CBT) with a purely operant paradigm (CM) for producing desired behavior change among substance-abusing clients with co-occurring ASPD. Furthermore, this study assesses the relative efficacy of combining these interventions (CBT+CM) for reducing cocaine use among methadone-maintained patients with ASPD. Since all patients are involved in a "platform" condition of methadone maintenance, it is possible to use a study design in which three active cocaine treatment conditions (CBT, CM, and CBT+CM) are compared to a control condition in which patients receive no additional treatment for their cocaine disorder.

Because of the limited literature (both in number and design) regarding substance abuse treatment responsivity for ASPD patients, findings are somewhat difficult to interpret. It is possible that group differences within the methadone maintenance studies have not been found because of the low power generated by the insufficient sample sizes. For example, it is likely that Brooner et al. (1998) would have found a significant difference between the ASPD patients in the experimental (CM) condition and the ASPD patients in the control condition had they used a larger sample. (By our calculations, their preliminary study generated a power of only .07, with an effect size of .15). The ASPD patients in the CM condition had a larger number of drug-free urine specimens, on average, than did the ASPD patients in the control condition. Monetary incentives for cocaine abstinence could be a strong external motivator for patients with ASPD.

Monetary incentives *combined* with drug-relapse education and peer support (i.e., CBT) might prove to be a strong treatment intervention for co-disordered patients.

Therefore, we hypothesized that ASPD patients in the three treatment conditions (CBT, CM, CBT+CM) would have better treatment responsivity over the 16-week course of treatment than would ASPD patients in the control condition (i.e., methadone maintenance only). Moreover, we hypothesized that there would be a cumulative treatment effect among ASPD patients over the course of treatment, with good performance in the CBT condition, better performance in the CM condition, and optimum performance in the CBT+CM condition.

$$[CBT] < [CM] < [CBT + CM]$$

Conversely, we hypothesized that the positive treatment effect of CM would decline for the ASPD patients once the incentive is removed (i.e., during the posttreatment outcome period). Because it has been speculated that ASPD patients have little internal motivation, it is reasonable to hypothesize that they will be less likely to remain abstinent in the absence of external incentives. Because the available literature assessing the relationship between ASPD and treatment outcomes is lacking, we also posed the more general research question: Is a diagnosis of ASPD a significant predictor of treatment outcomes?

METHOD

The data for this study is from the "Behavioral/Cognitive Behavioral Trial for Cocaine

Abuse Project", a treatment outcome study for methadone-maintained, cocaine-dependent patients. The main treatment outcome report for this project can be found in Rawson et al. (2002). The current chapter focuses on the ASPD diagnosis and its relation to treatment outcomes.

Patients

Study participants were volunteers from two licensed narcotic treatment programs in Los Angeles, California (Matrix Institute and West Los Angeles Treatment Program). To be eligible for the study, all candidates were required: (1) to have been on methadone maintenance treatment at one of the two clinics for a minimum of 90 days; (2) to meet DSM-IV criteria for cocaine dependence; and (3) to show evidence of cocaine use (cocaine-metabolite positive urine sample) during the month prior to study enrollment. Individuals were ineligible if they (1) were also dependent upon alcohol or benzodiazepines to the point of requiring withdrawal medication; (2) if they had received specific treatment for cocaine in the previous 30 days; or (3) if they were court-mandated to treatment.

During a 30-month recruitment period, 120 individuals met study eligibility criteria, were enrolled in the study, and were randomly assigned into one of the four study conditions (CBT, CM, CBT+CM, or MM). [2] At admission, slightly more than half (56%) of the sample was male and the mean age was 43. With respect to race/ethnicity, 38% of the sample were White, 31% African American, 28% Hispanic, and 6% "other." The majority of patients (72%) had completed at least 12 years of school. A small percentage (15%) of the sample reported that they had steady employment over the past 3 years. Among the four conditions, none of the between-group differences in patient characteristics was statistically significant. Similar to the demographic profiles, self-reported prevalence of past-month drug and alcohol use did not vary significantly by study condition.

Procedures

Random assignment into one of the four study conditions (30 patients in each condition) took place following informed consent procedures and a 2-week baseline data collection period.

Demographic and background information was captured using the Addiction Severity Index (ASI). The ASI is a semi-structured interview instrument used for both clinical and research purposes to determine service needs (McLellan et al., 1992). It is a comprehensive instrument consisting of questions pertaining to demographics, employment, living situation, past and current health status, past and current drug use, past and current drug treatment history, past and current criminal and criminal justice involvement, and past and current mental health status and treatment.

The Structural Clinical Interview for Mental Disorders-IV (SCID) was administered during the first 30 days of study participation by a trained masters- or Ph.D.-level staff person to confirm the substance use diagnosis and to determine the presence of ASPD. The SCID is a semi-structured interview

---

[2] Only four individuals volunteered for study participation in the first 60 days of recruitment. The two study clinics operated on a fee-for-service basis in which patients paid either $140 (Matrix Clinic) or $180 (West LA Clinic) per month for methadone maintenance treatment services. Only after a $40 per month methadone program fee-reduction was offered as an incentive for study participation did study recruitment become adequate. Thus, the group of individuals who participated in this study can be characterized as having relatively low motivation to stop their cocaine use as defined by the requirement of a $40 per month incentive to encourage study participation.

for making Axis I and Axis II diagnoses based on DSM-IV criteria (Kranzler, Rounsaville, & Tennen, 1995). SCID interviews were supervised and reviewed by a Ph.D.-level staff member. A total of 108 clients were evaluated by the SCID diagnostic interview and are the focus of this study (12 patients dropped-out of treatment prior to administration of the SCID). Forty-four percent of the target sample met the DSM-IV criteria for ASPD. The frequency of ASPD among the study patients is consistent with other reports on the psychiatric co-morbidity among methadone maintained-individuals (Rounseville, Eyre, Weissman, & Kleber, 1983; Sievewright & Daly, 1997).

Treatment Interventions

CBT procedures. The CBT procedure consisted of a total of 48 group sessions (3 per week for 16 weeks). Typical groups had four to eight patients. Each group session was scheduled to be 90 minutes in duration, and the material for each session was provided in a workbook. Each workbook presented a concept or a brief written exercise that explained or illustrated an aspect of cognitive-behavioral therapy. This method has been found in previous work by Rawson, Obert, McCann, Smith, and Scheffey (1989) to help stimulant users achieve and maintain abstinence. Many of the concepts were distilled from Marlatt and Gordon (1985) and/or are consistent with the National Institute on Drug Abuse manual on CBT (Carroll, 1999). Each session was led by a master's level therapist who had received 40-60 hours of supervised training in delivering the materials in a standardized manner. All sessions were audiotaped and reviewed by a counseling supervisor. Feedback was given to the therapist to shape and reinforce consistency.

The session format consisted of the topic being introduced by the staff member/group leader, the sheet being read aloud by the leader or a participant volunteer, and group members being given approximately 5 to 10 minutes to discuss the relevance of the topic to him/herself. Those individuals who were unwilling to discuss the topic were allowed to sit and listen. At the end of the topic discussion (typically 45-60 minutes into the session), each individual was asked to discuss his/her drug use/nonuse over the previous time period since the last group. The group leader and other group members verbally reinforced those reporting no use, less use, and/or the initiation of some new prosocial behavior. Finally, each member was asked to describe his/her behavioral plan for the time period leading up to the next session. Plans that included activities based upon the cognitive behavioral principles presented in the treatment groups received praise from the group leader and other members.

CM procedures. Patients in the CM-only condition were required to provide three urine samples per week and meet briefly (2-5 minutes) with the CM technician. The meetings with the CM technician covered four topics: (1) a review of the results of the urine test (tested immediately using enzyme multiplied immunoassay tests [EMIT]); (2) the delivery of the appropriate paper voucher certificate, if earned; (3) a discussion of how the voucher or accumulated voucher account could be redeemed; and (4) the delivery of the earned items when the vouchers were redeemed. On occasions when vouchers were earned, the CM technician provided praise and encouragement for successful performance. Patients who provided samples positive for stimulants (there were no contingencies for drug use other than stimulants) were not "scolded" or punished (other than the punishment of withholding the voucher).

The voucher value was based upon an escalating schedule that was similar to that used in previous studies (Higgins et al., 1993, 1994). The initial voucher value started at $2.50 per stimulant-negative sample, increasing in value by $1.25 with each successive negative sample, and with a $10 bonus for three consecutive stimulant-negative samples. The maximum voucher value was $46.25 per sample (excluding the $10 bonus). Across the course of the entire 16 weeks, the maximum possible earning (48 consecutive stimulant-free samples) was $1,277.50. Cash was never given to patients. As the voucher account increased in value as a result of stimulant-free urine samples, patients were encouraged to "spend" their savings on items that could support drug-free activities.

Patients in all study conditions received identical methadone maintenance (MM) services. The average dose of methadone at baseline was 72 milligrams for the CBT group, 62 milligrams for the CM group, 68 milligrams for the CBT+CM group, and 71 milligrams for the MM-only group. Participation in the study had no effect on the nature of their MM treatment. There were very clear rules for the termination of patients from the study. Termination could be a result of: (1) study completion (16-weeks); (2) missing two consecutive weekly data collection visits; or (3) missing either six consecutive CBT groups or six consecutive urine samples. Therefore, a consistent 2-week absence from protocol participation was the criterion for study termination across all study conditions.

Study Measures

The cocaine treatment intervention lasted 16 weeks for all conditions. Cocaine use, as measured by urinalysis, was the principal dependent measure during and after treatment. All study patients were required to give three urine samples per week throughout the 16-week study period and at each of the three follow-up interviews (17, 26, and 52 weeks). All samples were analyzed for metabolites of cocaine (benzoylecognine, BE) and methamphetamine. (Methamphetamine was included as a target along with cocaine to prevent "stimulant switching"; however, the frequency of methamphetamine use in this population was almost nonexistent. Hence, the study findings are specific to cocaine). A 300 ng/ml urinary BE cutoff was used to define a positive sample. All samples were analyzed on-site using EMIT (SYVA) reagent test procedures. All samples were monitored (i.e., collected in bottles equipped with temperature strips, and the bathrooms where samples were collected did not have hot water to prevent tampering). In addition, approximately 33% of all samples were collected under observation. Observation of urine specimens was conducted on a random basis. All subjects were breath alcohol tested at the time of the collection of each urine sample.

Follow-up urine specimens were analyzed for cocaine, methamphetamine, metabolites of illicit opiates, benzodiazepines, barbiturates, and cannabinoids. Ninety percent of the sample provided urine specimens at the 17-week follow-up, 83% provided specimens at the 26-week follow-up, and 83% provided specimens at the 52-week follow-up. There were no significant differences in follow-up rates between those with and those without ASPD across the four study conditions at any of the follow-up periods (percentages shown below).

- *17-Week Follow-Up*: Non-ASPD CBT = 86%; ASPD CBT = 93%; Non-ASPD CM = 92%; ASPD CM = 93%; Non-ASPD CBT+CM = 89%; ASPD CBT+CM = 100%; Non- ASPD control = 87%; ASPD control = 83%.
- *26-Week Follow-Up*: Non-ASPD CBT = 79%; ASPD CBT = 93%; Non-ASPD CM = 83%; ASPD CM = 87%; Non-ASPD CBT+CM = 89%; ASPD CBT+CM = 86%; Non-ASPD control = 73%; ASPD control = 75%.

Data Analysis

The distribution of demographic and drug-use characteristics by ASPD status was evaluated using chi-square analysis and t-tests. Similarly, the distribution of SCID-I and II diagnoses across study conditions was evaluated by chi-square analysis. In-treatment cocaine use measures were analyzed using a Two-Way Analysis of Variance (ANOVA). To control for inflated alpha error, Tukey-Kramer tests were used for all post hoc comparisons. In addition, a series of regression analyses were conducted to assess in-treatment cocaine use while controlling for pre-existing differences between those with and those without ASPD.

Table 1. Sample Characteristics at Admission, by ASPD Status (N = 108)

	No ASPD (N = 60)	ASPD (N = 48)	Total (N = 108)
Characteristics	%	%	%
Gender			
Male	43**	71**	56
Female	57	29	44
	100%	100%	100%
Race/Ethnicity			
White	43	31	38
Black	40**	21**	31
Hispanic/Other	17	48	31
	100%	100%	100%
Mean Age at Admission (SD)	43.7 (7.6)	43.5 (8.1)	43
Education			
Less than 12 years	18*	40*	28
High-school Degree or more	82	60	72
	100%	100%	100%
Full Time Employment Past 3 Years	17	13	15
Study Condition			
CBT	23	29	26
CM	20	31	25
CBT+CM	32	15	24
MM	25	25	25
	100%	100%	100%

*p < .05. **p < .01.
52-Week Follow-Up: Non-ASPD CBT = 79%; ASPD CBT = 86%; Non-ASPD CM = 75%; ASPD CM = 93%; Non-ASPD CBT+CM = 95%; ASPD CBT+CM = 71%; Non-ASPD control = 73%; ASPD control = 83%.

To assess cocaine and heroin use following treatment, separate chi-square analyses were conducted for those with and those without ASPD at each of the follow-up time periods. All statistical tests were considered significant at $p \leq$ .05 and were two-tailed.

RESULTS

Demographic characteristics for ASPD and non-ASPD patients were similar across the four study conditions; however, small cell sizes limited reliable statistical inference. Although patients were randomly assigned to the study conditions, they were not randomly assigned by ASPD diagnosis. To further explore any pre-existing differences, all ASPD patients were compared with all non-ASPD patients with regard to their demographic and drug use characteristics.

**Table 2. Self-Reported Drug/Alcohol Use 30 Days Prior to Admission,
by ASPD Status (N = 108)**

	No ASPD (N = 60)	ASPD (N = 48)	Total (N = 108)
Substance Use 30 Days Prior to Admission	%	%	%
Alcohol Use	57	60	58
Alcohol Use to Intoxication	23	35	29
Marijuana	30	27	29
Heroin Use	58*	79*	68
Other Opiates	08**	31**	18
Cocaine Use	100	98	99
Amphetamines	03	08	06

*p < .05. **p < .01.

Consistent with previous literature, patients diagnosed with ASPD were significantly more likely to be male (71% vs. 43%, $p < .01$) and to have less than a high school education (40% vs. 18%, $p < .05$) than non-ASPD patients (see Table 1). With regard to ethnicity, patients with ASPD were significantly more likely than non-ASPD patients to be Hispanic (48% vs. 17%, $p < .01$). No significant differences between those with and those without ASPD were found with regard to age or employment, and patients with ASPD were equally distributed among the study conditions.

Table 3. SCID-I and II Diagnoses, by Study Condition (N = 108)[a]

Diagnoses[b]	CBT (N=28)	CM (N=27)	CBT+CM (N=26)	MM (N=27)	Total (N=108)
SCID-I					
Substance Use Disorder	100	100	100	100	100
Mood Disorder	18	33	23	19	23
Anxiety Disorder	18	37	27	19	25
SCID-II					
Antisocial Personality Disorder (ASPD)	50	56	27	44	44
All Diagnoses					
Substance Use Disorder Only	29	23	50	36	34
Substance Use and Other Axis I Disorders	21	22	23	19	21
Substance Use and ASPD	36	22	12	26	24
Substance Use, ASPD, and Other Axis I Dis.	14	33	15	19	21
	100%	100%	100%	100%	100%

[a] N's vary slightly due to missing data.
[b] Only diagnoses prevalent in 5% or more of the sample are shown.
Note. Differences are not significant.

Comparisons of demographic characteristics of *ASPD-patients only* across the four study conditions were also conducted. No significant differences were found with regard to age, gender, race/ethnicity, or high school education (results are not shown).

Table 2 displays the self-reported drug and alcohol use patterns by ASPD status during the 30 days prior to study admission. Those with ASPD were significantly more likely to have used heroin (79% vs. 58%, $p < .05$) and other opiates (31% vs. 8%, $p < .01$) during this time period, than non-ASPD patients. No other substance-use differences were found. Cocaine (99%) and heroin (68%) were most likely to be used during the 30 days prior to study admission, followed by alcohol (58%), marijuana (29%), other opiates (18%), and amphetamines (6%).

Table 3 displays the prevalence of ASPD, substance use disorder, and other SCID-I psychiatric disorders by study condition. Only those diagnoses prevalent in more than 5% of the sample are shown. There were no significant differences among the four study conditions with regard to prevalence of psychiatric disorders. All subjects met the criteria for substance use disorder and almost half (44%) had co-occurring ASPD. Of those evaluated by the SCID, 34% had no disorders other than substance use, 21% had substance use and other Axis I disorders, 24% had substance use with co-occurring ASPD, and 21% had substance use disorder, co-occurring ASPD, and other Axis I disorders. (All analyses combine clients with substance use disorder only and those with other Axis I disorders into the non-ASPD group.)

In-Treatment Performance

Treatment retention. Treatment retention is frequently an important outcome indicator and is sometimes used as one measure of treatment efficacy. In this study, the value of treatment retention as a dependent measure was compromised by the necessity to reduce patients' monthly methadone program fees by $40 to promote study enrollment. Therefore, not surprisingly, there was no significant difference in study retention for patients with and those without ASPD across four study conditions. The average number of weeks in treatment for the ASPD group was 14.7 (SD = 3.4), ranging from 12 to 16. The average number of weeks in treatment for the non-ASPD group was 13.2 (SD = 4.9), ranging from 10 to 15 weeks.

Cocaine-abstinence during treatment. The primary dependent measure in this study was cocaine use as measured by urine toxicology. Since retention in treatment was not significantly different for those with and without ASPD across study conditions, the most direct measure of cocaine use across the 16 weeks of the trial was the number of *cocaine-negative* urine samples given by each participant during their 48 opportunities to give samples (3 times per week for 16 weeks). There were no significant differences between those with and those without ASPD across the four study conditions with regard to the rates of missing urines.

A Two-Way ANOVA was performed to determine differences in the mean number of cocaine-negative samples (CNS) provided by ASPD status and by study condition. The possibility of an interaction effect (ASPD status X study condition) was also explored. We initially asked if ASPD would be a significant predictor of in-treatment responsivity. There was a significant main effect for ASPD status. The mean number of CNS for patients with ASPD (CNS = 27.4, SD = 17.5) was significantly higher than the mean number of CNS for those without ASPD (CNS = 20.5, SD = 19.4) [F (1,107) = 4.74, p < .05), suggesting that ASPD patients performed better during the 16-week treatment course than non-ASPD patients. However, there was no interaction effect between ASPD status and study condition.

We also hypothesized that ASPD patients in the three cocaine treatment conditions (CBT, CM, CBT+CM) would have better outcomes than ASPD patients in the control condition (MM). This hypothesis was supported. Pairwise comparisons of the mean number of CNS indicated that ASPD patients in each of the treatment conditions had significantly higher scores than those in the control condition (CBT = 24.8; CM = 39.4; CBT+CM = 37.7; vs. MM = 9.3, p < .05). The same pattern was found among the study conditions for the non-ASPD group, but differences were not statistically significant (see Table 4).

The above findings indicate that ASPD patients responded positively to the three cocaine treatment conditions; however, we also hypothesized a cumulative treatment effect for ASPD patients, with optimum performance in the CBT+CM condition (CBT< CM < CBT+CM).

Table 4. Treatment Effectiveness Scores for In-Treatment Cocaine-Free Urine Samples, by Study Condition and ASPD Status

ASPD Status	CBT	CM*	CBT+CM	MM
No ASPD Mean TES for Cocaine (s.d)	17.6 (17.9)$_a$	25.5 (20.7)$_a$	24.2 (21.1)$_a$	14.5 (16.9)$_a$
ASPD Mean TES for Cocaine (S.D.)	24.8 (15.6)$_a$	39.4 (11.4)$_b$	37.7 (13.3)$_{ab}$	9.3 (11.3)$_c$

Note. Subscripts represent the results of pairwise comparisons between study conditions; means that *do not* have a subscript in common are significantly different from each other (p < .05).

*The CM condition was the only condition with a significant difference between those with and without ASPD (p < .05).

This hypothesis was not supported. Pairwise comparisons did show that the mean number of CNS for the ASPD patients in the CM condition was significantly higher than the mean number of CNS for the ASPD patients in the CBT-only condition (CBT = 24.8 vs. CM = 39.4, p < .05). However, no differences were found for the ASPD patients in the CBT+CM condition compared with the ASPD patients in the CM or CBT-only groups (shown in Table 4).

Moreover, ASPD patients in the CM condition performed significantly better than the non-ASPD CM patients (ASPD/CM CNS = 39.4 vs. non-ASPD/CM CNS = 25.5, p < .05). The differences in CNS means were not significant for ASPD and non-ASPD patients in any of the other study conditions (shown in Figure 1).

The above bivariate analyses, however, do not take into account pre-existing differences between those with and without ASPD that might be related to in-treatment performance. Initially, no demographic differences were found between those with and those without ASPD in any of the treatment conditions; however, when we compared *all* of the ASPD patients with *all* of the non-ASPD patients (see Tables 1 and 2), some pre-existing differences were evident (i.e., gender, race, high school education, and opiate use).

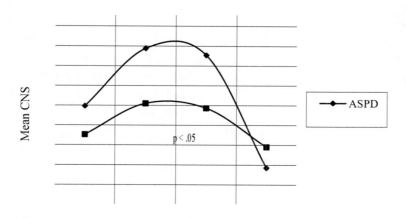

Study Conditions

Figure 1. Cocaine-Negative Specimens Provided During Treatment (N=108).

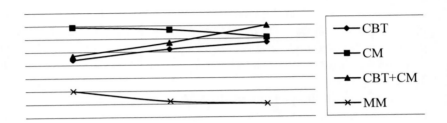

Follow-Up Time Periods

Figure 2. Cocaine-Free Urine Specimens During Follow-Up [ASPD Patients].

Therefore, we decided to further explore the association of ASPD with CM treatment using multivariate analyses. Because the total number of patients in the CM condition fell below 30, we were limited in the number of independent variables (or predictors) that could be included in the multivariate analyses (Keppel, 1991). Thus, we conducted a series of regressions pairing ASPD with each of the above characteristics. In all of these pairings, a diagnosis of ASPD remained significantly related to the mean number of CNS (p<.01). We further confirmed the *lack* of an association of ASPD to in-treatment performance among the other study conditions (analyses not shown).

Post-Treatment Performance

Cocaine urinalysis results for ASPD patients at each follow-up period. We hypothesized that the positive treatment effect of CM would decline for the ASPD patients once the incentives were removed (i.e., no vouchers were given during the posttreatment outcome periods). This hypothesis was not supported. ASPD patients in the CM conditions continued to abstain from cocaine use throughout the three follow-up time periods. Figure 2 shows that ASPD patients in the CM-only condition were as likely as those in the other study conditions to have cocaine-free urine specimens at weeks 17, 26, and 52. In fact, over 70% of the CM-only group provided cocaine-free specimens at each follow-up time period. Overall, differences in percentages of cocaine-free specimens between the treatment groups and the control group were not significant at weeks 17 and 26. However, percentages were significantly different at week 52, indicating that between 65% and 80% of the ASPD patients in any of the three treatment conditions were abstaining from cocaine use at the 52-week follow-up period, compared to 20% in the control condition ($\underline{p} < .05$).

Cocaine urinalysis results for non-ASPD patients at each follow-up period. The rates of cocaine abstinence for the non-ASPD patients did not follow the same trends as those for the ASPD patients. Figure 3 shows that the percentages of cocaine-free specimens were similar across the four study groups for each follow-up time period (i.e., no significant differences were found). However, the CBT-only group was the only treatment group that showed substantial increases in abstinence over the three follow-up time periods (33%, 64%, and 81% respectively).

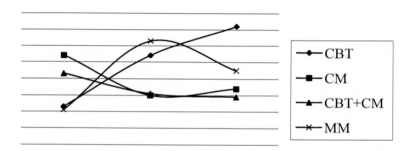

Follow-Up Time Periods

Figure 3. Cocaine-Free Urine Specimens During Follow-Up [Non-ASPD Patients].

Post-treatment responsivity. To assess overall differences in posttreatment performance between those with and those without ASPD, we created a posttreatment responsivity measure that totaled the percentages of patients who had cocaine-free urine specimens at all three of the follow-up periods. Figure 4 shows the posttreatment results by study condition for those with and those without ASPD. Among non-ASPD patients, there were no significant differences in cocaine negative specimens at each of the three follow-up time periods.

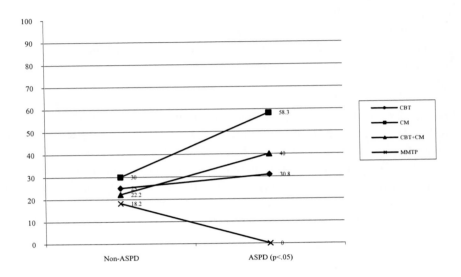

Figure 4. Percentage of Cocaine-Free Urine Specimens at All Three Follow-Up Periods (N=91).

In contrast, the ASPD patients in the three cocaine treatment conditions showed large differences in continued abstinence from cocaine compared with those in the control condition ($p < .05$). Over half of the ASPD patients in the CM-only condition had cocaine-free urine results at each follow-up interview (58%), followed by those in the CBT+CM condition (40%), and those in the CBT-only condition (31%). None of the MM-only group had three consecutive cocaine-free urine results.

Because the posttreatment findings regarding cocaine use were not as expected, we explored the possibility that ASPD patients were more likely than non-ASPD patients to be using heroin at the follow-up time periods. These results are shown below.

Post-treatment heroin urinalysis results. Overall, study patients were less likely to abstain from heroin use, compared to cocaine use, at the three follow-up time periods regardless of treatment group or ASPD status (see Figures 5 and 6). However, abstinence rates were not trivial. At the 26-week follow-up, between 40% and 50% of the ASPD patients tested negative for heroin, whereas between 50% and 60% of the non-ASPD patients tested negative for heroin. In addition, non-ASPD patients in the CBT-only condition were significantly more likely to abstain from heroin at the 17-week follow-up compared with those in the other treatment conditions (CBT = 75% vs. CM = 36% vs. CBT+CM = 35% vs. MM = 23%, p < .05).

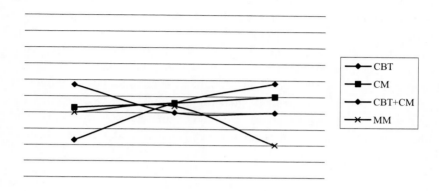

Follow-Up Time Periods

Figure 5. Heroin-Free Urine Specimens During Follow-Up [ASPD Participants].

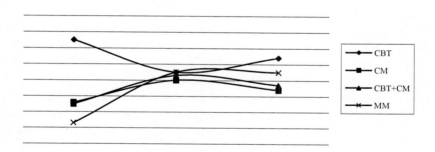

Follow-Up Time Periods

Figure 6. Heroin-Free Urine Specimens During Follow-Up [Non-ASPD Participants].

CONCLUSION

Recent findings of successful treatment outcomes for methadone-maintained patients with ASPD provides a strong argument against the perception that substance abusers with ASPD are unresponsive to drug treatment (Brooner et al., 1998; Gil et al., 1992; Silverman et al., 1998). However, these studies have been limited by small sample sizes and ambiguous designs. The current study sought to overcome the limitations of the previous research. The primary goal of this study was to determine the efficacy of two commonly used treatment approaches, separately and combined, for the treatment of cocaine dependence in methadone-maintained patients with co-occurring ASPD.

In-Treatment Responsivity

Three major trends of in-treatment responsivity are evident. First, in contrast to previous findings (and beliefs), we found that a diagnosis of ASPD was significantly and positively related to treatment responsivity. Those with ASPD were more likely to abstain from cocaine use during treatment than those without ASPD. Second, ASPD patients in each of the treatment conditions performed significantly better than ASPD patients in the control condition, whereas no differences in performance by study condition were found for the non-ASPD patients. Third, the strong treatment effect for ASPD patients was primarily due to the CM condition. During the 16-week course of treatment, those in the CM condition were significantly more likely to abstain from cocaine use than those in the CBT-only condition. In contrast, abstinence levels in the combined treatment group (CBT+CM) fell between the CBT- and CM-only levels and did not differ significantly from either. Furthermore, ASPD patients in the CM condition were significantly more likely to abstain from cocaine use than non-ASPD patients in the CM condition, even after controlling for pre-existing differences.

As earlier theorists hypothesized (Evans & Sullivan, 1990; Valliant, 1975), monetary incentives appear to be a successful treatment intervention for reducing cocaine use among substance abusers with co-occurring ASPD, and a more successful intervention than for those without ASPD. Furthermore, patients with ASPD responded significantly better to this type of intervention than ASPD patients in "talk-based therapy." The larger question, however, was whether the positive treatment effects of the CM intervention would continue beyond the course of treatment, once the incentive was removed.

Post-Treatment Responsivity

Four major results are evident from our posttreatment outcomes. First, and contrary to our hypothesis, ASPD patients in the CM conditions continued to abstain from cocaine use throughout the three follow-up periods. Although differences in cocaine abstinence between the groups were not significant, ASPD patients in the CM conditions appeared to maintain the highest levels of posttreatment cocaine abstinence. In addition, comparable numbers of ASPD and non-ASPD patients were abstaining from heroin at the follow-up time periods. Second, ASPD patients in all three treatment conditions were significantly more likely to abstain from cocaine use at the 52 week follow-up than those in the control condition. Third, a clear pattern of posttreatment performance between the treatment groups was not evident for the non-ASPD patients. Non-ASPD patients in the CM conditions appeared to do well at the first follow-up, but their performance declined substantially during the remaining follow-up periods. In contrast, non-ASPD patients in the CBT-only group were the only treatment group whose performance increased over the follow-up time periods. And fourth, ASPD patients in each of the treatment conditions were significantly more likely to test negative for cocaine at *all* three of the follow-up periods than those in the MM-only condition, whereas no differences were found for non-ASPD patients. Most importantly, ASPD patients in the CM condition were twice as likely as non-ASPD patients in the CM condition to have negative urine test results for cocaine at all follow-up periods.

These findings provide a strong argument against the perception that substance abusers with ASPD are unresponsive to drug treatment. Consequently, these findings are important in light of treatment program exclusionary criteria and current public policy. Many substance abuse treatment programs across the nation exclude persons with ASPD on the assumption that they will not respond well to treatment efforts (Messina et al., 1999). Furthermore, a diagnosis of ASPD is among the exclusionary criteria for Maryland's newly constructed Public Mental Health System, and ASPD is the only personality diagnosis deemed untreatable within this system of health service delivery (Brooner et al., 1998). The results of the present study and other recent publications suggest that substance abusers with ASPD may be more responsive to treatment than previously believed.

Study Strengths

The primary strength of our study was the rigorous study design. Random assignment of patients across study conditions created comparable groups. As a result, any differences between group performance tend to reflect the effect of the treatment intervention, rather than error variance (Bordens & Abbott, 1991). Random assignment also eliminated the issue of self-selection, which can be affected by such client attributes as personal motivation, perception of treatment modality, and treatment availability (Hser, 1995). In addition, the "platform" condition of methadone maintenance made it possible to use a study design with a true control condition.

Another strength of our study was the high prevalence rate of ASPD (45%), which is similar to other estimates of ASPD among methadone-maintained patients (ranging from 25% to 54%; Rounsaville, Eyre, Weissman, & Kleber, 1983). The high prevalence of this disorder within our sample allowed us to make comparisons of ASPD patients across study conditions, as well as between those with and those without ASPD. Thus, we were able to assess the treatment responsivity of ASPD patients in each treatment condition and compare their performance to those without ASPD.

The use of objective measures of drug use to assess treatment outcomes was an additional strength of this study. Self-reported drug use may be considerably less valid than previously reported (Messina, Wish, Nemes, & Wraight, 2000). For example, Wish, Hoffman, and Nemes (1997) found that among substance-abusing populations, clients were more likely to truthfully report heroin use than cocaine use. The authors further suggest that self-reports may be less valid at follow-up than at intake.

Study Limitations

Some limitations of this study should also be kept in mind when interpreting the results. The primary limitation is the sample size. Although our study had a larger sample than previous research among methadone-maintained patients, our posttreatment comparisons were limited by small cell sizes due to the four study conditions. However, we were able to improve power as compared to our calculations for Brooner's (1998) study. (Power calculation for our study =.47, effect size = .37; power calculation for Brooner = .07, effect size = .15).

Another limitation of this study (and others) is the existence of other psychiatric disorders among the sample. Patients with and without ASPD may have been diagnosed with various other psychiatric disorders. It is difficult to know the degree to which the various combinations of other disorders confounded the distinction between those with and those without ASPD, or if the presence of additional psychiatric disorders in patients with ASPD moderates the effect of the ASPD diagnosis on treatment response. However, recent findings from a large sample of methadone-maintained patients (N = 518) demonstrated minor differences between patients with ASPD only and patients with ASPD and other psychiatric disorders (King, Kidorf, Stoller, Carter, & Brooner, 2001). ASPD-only patients exhibited higher rates of heroin use during treatment, whereas ASPD patients with additional disorders exhibited higher rates of benzodiazepine use. No differences between the two groups were found for cocaine use during treatment.

An additional roadblock facing those who study and treat ASPD is the lack of agreement about a basic definition and the use of different definitions. There is much controversy among social scientists and clinicians over the proper measurement of ASPD among substance abusers. Although social scientists most often use diagnostic interviews that follow DSM-IV criteria to assess ASPD (such as the SCID-II), many have raised concerns about possible limitations of the DSM (Messina, Wish, Hoffman, & Nemes, 2001). It has been suggested that the DSM criteria for ASPD focus on behavioral characteristics instead of underlying personality traits and do not require that ASPD occur independently of substance abuse (Gerstley et al., 1990). Rounsaville et al. (1983) suggest that clients whose antisocial activities are independent of the need to obtain drugs are "primary antisocial addicts" and those whose antisocial activities are directly related to drug use are "secondary antisocial addicts." The authors speculated that secondary antisocial addicts might have better treatment responses. If most of our sample members were secondary antisocial addicts, it could account for their more positive treatment outcomes.

Summary

The relationships between ASPD, substance abuse, and crime is the nexus of a major social problem and understanding the interactions among these patterns of behavior will help identify the individuals and groups who most need effective intervention. The findings from the current study and other recent literature indicate that substance abusers with co-occurring ASPD can benefit from drug treatment programs. Furthermore, methadone-maintained ASPD patients participating in CM interventions show substantial reductions in cocaine use beyond the intervention period. It is therefore suggested that treatment programs make efforts to attract and retain substance abusers with a diagnosis of ASPD. Future research should continue to explore the many issues surrounding the diagnosis of ASPD, as well as its relationship to treatment outcomes.

ACKNOWLEDGMENTS

We are grateful to the staff and the patients at the Matrix Institute and the West Los Angeles Treatment Program for their participation. We would like to thank Alice Huber, Christie Thomas, Vikas Gulati, Al Hasson, and Michael McCann for their assistance with the conduct of this study.

REFERENCES

American Psychiatric Association (APA). (1994). *Diagnostic and Statistical Manual of Mental Disorders, 4th Edition (DSM-IV)*. Washington, DC.

Abram, K. M. (1989). The effect of co-occurring disorders on criminal career: Interaction of antisocial personality, alcoholism, and drug disorders. *International Journal of Law and Psychiatry, 12*, 133-148.

Bandura, A. (1977). Self-efficacy: Toward a unifying theory of behavioral change. *Psychological Review, 84,* 191-215.

Bordens, K., & Abbott, B. (1991). *Research design and methods: A process approach* (2nd Ed.). Mountain View, CA: Mayfield Publishing Company.

Brooner, R., Kidorf, M., King, V., & Stoller, K. (1998). Preliminary evidence of good treatment response in antisocial drug abusers. *Drug and Alcohol Dependence, 49,* 249-260.

Brooner, R., Schmidt, C., Felch, L., & Bigelow, G. (1992). Antisocial behavior of intravenous drug abusers: Implications for diagnosis of antisocial personality disorder. *American Journal of Psychiatry, 149,* 482-487.

Carroll, K. (Ed.) (1999). A cognitive-behavioral approach: Treating cocaine addiction. *Therapy Manuals for Drug Addiction.* Rockville, MD: National Institute on Drug Abuse, U.S. Department of Health and Human Services, National Institutes of Health.

Carroll, K.M., Rounsaville, B.J., Nich, C., Gordon, L.T., Wirtz, P.W., & Gawin, F.H. (1994). One year follow-up of psychotherapy and pharmacotherapy for cocaine dependence: Delayed emergence of psychotherapy effects. *Archives of General Psychiatry,* 51, 989-997.

Coon, Dennis. (1983) *Introduction to Psychology: Exploration and Application.* 3rd ed. Los Angeles: West Publishing Company.

Davison, G. C., & Neale, J. M. (1990). *Abnormal psychology* (5th ed.). New York: Wiley & Sons.

Evans, K., & Sullivan, J. (1990*). Dual diagnoses: Counseling mentally ill substance abusers.* New York: The Guilford Press.

Everingham, S., & Rydell, C. (1994). *Modeling the demand for cocaine.* Santa Monica, CA: RAND.

Farabee, D., Rawson, R., & McCann, M. (2002). Adoption of drug avoidance activities among patients in contingency management and cognitive-behavioral treatments. *Journal of Substance Abuse Treatment, 23,* 343-350.

Foote, J., Seligman, M., Magura, S., Handelsman, L., Rosenblum, A., Lovejoy, M., Arrington, K., & Stimmel, B. (1994). An enhanced positive reinforcement model for the severely impaired cocaine abuser. *Journal of Substance Abuse Treatment, 11*(6), 525-539.

Forrest, G. G. (1992). *Chemical dependency and antisocial personality disorder: Psychotherapy and assessment strategies.* New York: The Hawthorne Press.

Gerstley, L. J., Alterman, A. I., McLellan, A. T., & Woody, G. E. (1990). Antisocial personality disorder in patients with substance abuse disorders: A problematic diagnosis? *American Journal of Psychiatry, 147*(2), 173-178.

Gil, K., Nolimal, D., & Crowley, T. (1992). Antisocial personality disorder, HIV risk behavior and retention in methadone maintenance therapy. *Drug and Alcohol Dependence, 30*(3), 247-252.

Higgins, T., Budney, J., Bickel, K., Foerg, F., Donham, R., & Badger, J. (1994). Incentives improve outcome in outpatient behavioral treatment of cocaine dependence. *Archives of General Psychiatry, 51*(7), 568-576.

Higgins, T., Budney, J., Bickel, K., Hughes, R., Foerg, F., & Badger, J. (1993). Achieving cocaine abstinence with a behavior approach. *American Journal of Psychiatry, 150*, 763-769.

Hser, Y. (1995). Drug treatment counselor practices and effectiveness: An examination of literature and relevant issues in a multilevel framework. *Evaluation Review, 19*(4), 389-408.

Keppel, G. (1991). *Design and analyses: A researcher's handbook*. Prentice Hall: Englewood Cliffs, New Jersey.

King, V., Kidorf, M., Stoller, M., Carter, J., & Brooner, R. (2001). Influence of antisocial personality subtypes on drug abuse treatment response. *Journal of Nervous and Mental Disease, 189*, 593-601.

Kranzler, H., Rounsaville, B., & Tennen, H. (1995). *Validity of the SCID in substance abuse patients* (NIDA Research Monograph, 2, 35). Rockville, MD: National Institute on Drug Abuse.

Marlatt, G. & Gordon, J. (Eds.). (1985). *Relapse prevention: Maintenance strategies in the treatment of addictive behaviors*. New York: Guilford Press.

McLellan, A.T., Kushner, H., Metzger, D., Peters, R., Smith, I., Grissom, G., Pettinati, H., & Argeriou, M. (1992). The fifth edition of the Addiction Severity Index. *Journal of Substance Abuse Treatment, 9*, 199-213.

Messina, N. (2002). The antisocial personality. In Levinson, D. (Ed.). *Encyclopedia of Crime and Punishment*, vol.1. Great Barrington, Mass.: Berkshire Reference Works.

Messina, N., Wish, E., Hoffman, J., & Nemes, S. (2001). Diagnosing antisocial personality disorder among substance abusers: The Structured Clinical Interview for the DSM-III-R versus the Millon Clinical Multiaxial Inventory. *The American Journal of Drug and Alcohol Abuse,27*(4), 699-717.

Messina, N., Wish, E., & Nemes, S. (1999). Therapeutic community treatment for substance abusers with antisocial personality disorder. *Journal of Substance Abuse Treatment, 17*(1-2), 121-128.

Messina, N., Wish, E., Nemes, S., & Wraight, B. (2000). Correlates of underreporting of post-discharge cocaine use among therapeutic community clients. *Journal of Drug Issues, 30*(1), 119-132.

Rawson, R., Huber, A., McCann, M., Shoptaw, S., Farabee, D., Reiber, C., & Ling, W. (2002). A comparison of contingency management and cognitive-behavioral approaches for cocaine dependent methadone maintained individuals. *Archives of General Psychiatry, 59,* 817-824.

Rawson, R., Obert, J., McCann, M., & Ling, W. (1991). Psychological approaches to the treatment of cocaine dependency. *Journal of Addictive Diseases, 11,* 97-120.

Rawson, R., Obert, J., McCann, M., Smith, P., and Scheffey, H. (1989). *The neurobehavioral treatment manual, Matrix.* Beverly Hills, CA.

Rounsaville, B., Eyre, S., Weissman, M., & Kleber, H. (1983). The antisocial opiate addict. In B. Stimmeo (Vol. Ed.). *Psychosocial constructs: Alcoholism and substance abuse,* (pp. 29-43). New York: Hawthorne Press.

Skinner, B. (1938). *The behavior of organisms: An experimental analysis.* Englewood Cliffs, NJ: Prentice-Hall.

Seivewright, N., & Daly, C. (1997). Personality disorder and drug use: A review. *Drug and Alcohol Review, 16,* 235-250.

Silverman, K., Chutuape, M.A., Bigelow, G., & Stitzer, M. (1999). Voucher-based reinforcement of cocaine abstinence in treatment-resistant methadone patients: Effects of reinforcement magnitude. *Psychopharmacology, 146,* 128-138.

Silverman, K., Higgins, S., Montoya, I., Cone, E., Schuster, C., & Preston, K. (1996). Sustained cocaine abstinence in methadone maintenance patients through voucher-based reinforcement therapy. *Archives of General Psychiatry, 53,* 409-415.

Silverman, K., Wong, C., Umbricht-Schneiter, A., Montoya, I., Schuster, C., & Preston, K. (1998). Broad beneficial effects of cocaine abstinence reinforcement among methadone patients. *Journal of Consulting and Clinical Psychology, 66*(5), 811-824.

Tims, F. M., DeLeon, G., & Jainchill, N. (Eds.). (1994). *Therapeutic community: Advances in research and application* (NIDA Research Monograph No.144). Rockville, MD: National Institute on Drug Abuse.

Valliant, G. (1975). Sociopathy as a human process: A viewpoint. *Archives of General Psychiatry, 32,* 178-183.

Wish, E., Hoffman, J., & Nemes, S. (1997). The validity of self-reports of drug use at treatment admission and at follow-up: Comparisons with urinalysis and hair assays. In L. Harris (Ed.), *The validity of self-reports: The implications for survey research* (NIDA Research Monograph No. 167, pp. 200-225). Rockville, MD: National Institute on Drug Abuse.

Woody, G., McLellan, A.T., Luborsky, L, & O'Brien, C. (1985). Sociopathy and psychotherapy outcome. *Archives of General Psychiatry, 42,* 1081-1086.

In: Substance Abuse among Adolescents   ISBN: 978-1-61122-933-2
Editor: Isabelle M. Giordano   © 2011 Nova Science Publishers, Inc.

Chapter 6

ASSESSING COGNITIVE PERFORMANCE IN CHRONIC STREET DRUG USERS

Natalie A. Ceballos[1], Jeff A. Cheek,
Rick Tivis and Sara Jo Nixon

Department of Behavioral Sciences, University of Minnesota
Medical School,
Duluth, MN 55812, USA
Department of Education, University of Oklahoma, Norman, OK 73019.
Statistically Speaking LLP, 5223 W. Crossridge Street, Meridian, ID
83642, USA
Department of Psychology, University of Kentucky,115 Kastle Hall,
Lexington, KY 40506, USA

ABSTRACT

Clinical literature has long contained reports of cognitive decrements among substance abusing/dependent patients. However, the direct effects of chronic street drug use have been understudied to date. The paucity of research in this arena may be due in part to the myriad of co-occurring

---

[1] Correspondence should be addressed to Natalie A. Ceballos, Ph.D.Department of Behavioral Sciences, University of Minnesota Medical School,1035 University Drive, 236 Medical School Building, Duluth, MN 55812, Phone (218) 726-8425, Fax (218) 726-7559, E-mail: nceballo@d.umn.edu.

factors observed in treatment-seeking abusers of illicit substances. Factors such as alcohol dependence, psychiatric co-morbidity and medical disorders may confound the scientific investigation of cognitive decrements. In addition, more sensitive assessment strategies may also be needed to detect and characterize the subtle cognitive decrements associated with chronic drug use. The current chapter outlines these issues and presents strategies for addressing these concerns in the clinical research setting. A controlled laboratory study, designed to disentangle the cognitive effects of chronic street drug use in substance abusing subgroups, is also presented. The results of this study identify decrements of cognitive efficiency during a sustained attention task in detoxified, abstinent participants with a history of abuse of/dependence upon street drugs. Findings are discussed in the context of current trends in street drug research and the potential application of laboratory findings to the recovery of street drug users.

INTRODUCTION

It has long been known that chronic substance abuse is associated with a decline in cognitive functioning. However, the direct effects of chronic use of street drugs has remained understudied to date, in part due to the myriad of experimental design obstacles that plague this area of research. The current chapter focuses on behavioral (neuropsychological) assessments of cognitive functioning in adult, chronic users of several common street drugs, including marijuana, cocaine, methamphetamine, club drugs, and prescription medications, with a specific focus on experimental issues that limit this area of research. These issues are presented by drug group, and a summary of relevant issues is provided at the end of this section. In addition, a controlled laboratory study is presented, which addresses the measurement of attentional functioning in a population of polysubstance abusers with a history of street drug use. Finally, the impact of these cognitive deficits on the treatment of street drug users is discussed.

MARIJUANA

Cannabis is among the most widely used street drugs, with approximately 141 million users, an estimated 2.5% of the world's population (Cosa e Silva, 2002; Green et al., 2003). Recent data indicate that, in the United States alone,

3.2 million people reported using marijuana on a daily or almost daily basis over a 12-month period in 2004 (Substance Abuse and Mental Health Services Administration, 2005). The principal psychoactive constituent of marijuana is delta-9-tetrahydrocannabinol (THC), which acts by binding to specific G-protein cannabinoid receptors in the brain, most markedly in the hippocampus, cerebellum and basal ganglia (Childers and Breivogel, 1998; Elphick and Egertova, 2001; Vik et al., 2004). In recent years, progression in the view of marijuana as a medicinal substance has sparked a steady increase in research on the cognitive effects of chronic marijuana use (Corey, 2005; Gonzalez et al., 2002).

Acutely, within 12 to 24 hours of initial abstinence, marijuana use is linked to neuropsychological decrements in attention, executive functioning, short-term memory, and psychomotor functioning (Pope et al., 1995; Vik et al., 2004). Despite these effects, studies designed primarily to examine the chronic effects of "harder" street drugs such as illicit stimulants or opiates often discount the concomitant use of marijuana. This approach is supported by a number of studies that report no THC-related neuropsychological or neurophysiological differences in marijuana users compared to community controls (Lyketsos et al., 1999; Patrick et al., 1997).

Clearly, the literature remains contentious regarding long-term effects of marijuana use. A recent review of this literature by Gonzalez and colleagues (2002) addressed this issue by examining 40 studies of non-acute cannabis effects published between 1968 and 2001. The authors observed marijuana-related performance deficits in the cognitive domains of attention/working memory in 45% of these articles, perceptual motor skills in 28%, abstraction/executive function in 27%, and simple reaction time in 27%. Deficits were also reported, albeit less frequently, in learning (7%) and verbal domains (7%). These diverse findings were attributed to variation study methodology. The issues raised by the Gonzalez et al. (2002) review are relevant to the study of all street drugs and include the specificity of drug of choice, documentation of other drug use, selection of an appropriate control group, use of meaningful and valid psychological tests, and verification of abstinence, medical and psychiatric history. However, other potential contributing factors exist, including differential potency of marijuana across the time span of the available literature. Although some studies have indicated only a 2-3% increase in potency in the period from 1970s to 1990s, other authors speculate that the increased availability of high quality marijuana, coupled with different methods of smoking the drug, may contribute to the aforementioned cognitive findings (Green et al., 2003; Hall and Swift, 2000).

Because the neuropsychological literature pertaining to marijuana use is largely equivocal (Gonzalez et al., 2002), previous research could be cited in support of a variety of experimental strategies in studies that focus on issues other than marijuana use. Oftentimes, the wide-spread prevalence of marijuana use makes the exclusion of such individuals impractical. To minimize the variability associated with the inclusion of marijuana users, some authors have relied on strict documentation of usage patterns and/or require short-term abstinence prior to testing. Previous reports by Pope and colleagues (1995) suggest that given appropriate abstinence periods (i.e., > 24 hours), chronic marijuana use may not significantly impair neuropsychological performance. Other studies have considered level of abstinence on a continuum, based on declining levels of THC metabolites over a specified abstinence period (Huestis and Cone, 1998; Pope et al., 2002).

As identified previously by Gonzalez et al. (2002), the selection of appropriate control groups is particularly important when dealing with a drug that is as widely used as marijuana. A traditional community control sample, composed of individuals who have never used marijuana, likely would not provide an appropriate comparison group in the majority of studies of street drug users. Individuals who have never used marijuana might differ significantly from street drug users on a wide variety of extraneous variables, introducing unwanted sources of variation into the study. Pope and colleagues (2002) address this issue by recruiting community controls with a history of infrequent marijuana use.

COCAINE

A naturally occurring substance derived from the coca plant, cocaine was once an ingredient in many patent medicines in the United States (Warner, 1993). Cocaine impacts a variety of neurotransmitter systems by blocking their reuptake mechanisms, including norepinephrine, dopamine and serotonin (Warner, 1993). A number of administration routes are used, depending on the form in which the drug is present (see Warner, 1993 for review). In its raw form, cocaine is extracted by chewing coca leaves, and this remains a popular route of administration in South America. As a hydrochloride powder, cocaine is frequently snorted; however, a smoke-able form of cocaine is created by the transformation of this substance into its alkaloid form (i.e., "crack"). Research in human participants has indicated that smoking crack results in blood levels of cocaine comparable to that of injecting this drug (Warner, 1993). The introduction of crack cocaine led to a significant increase in the prevalence of cocaine use during the early 1980s (Cornish and O'Brien, 1996; Rogers and Robbins, 2001; Warner, 1993).

With respect to cocaine-related cognitive deficits, Simon et al. (2002a) reported verbal recall deficits in a sample of *current* cocaine users. O'Malley and colleagues (1992) reported neuropsychological deficits in a group of chronic cocaine abusers on a number of standard neuropsychological assessments including the Halstead Category Test, the Symbol Digit Modalities Test, and the WAIS-R Arithmetic Test of verbal memory. Further, the degree of deficiency was related to the amount and recency of cocaine use. Berry and colleagues (1993) reported impairments in memory, visuospatial abilites, and concentration within the first 72-hours of cocaine abstinence. Some deficits persisted after two weeks of abstinence. Beatty and colleagues (1995) examined cocaine abusers with 3 to 5 weeks of abstinence and found poorer performance relative to controls on measures of learning and memory, problem solving and abstraction and perceptual motor speed. Interestingly, no significant differences were noted for sustained attention. It has been hypothesized that the cerebrovascular impairment associated with cocaine use may be largely responsible for the persistence of such cognitive deficits (Strickland and Stein, 1995).

One significant issue that impacts the study of neuropsychological deficits in cocaine using populations is the frequent co-abuse of other substances. For instance, based on cost and availability, cocaine users often substitute illicit stimulants such as methamphetamine. Involuntary supplementation may also occur, as some studies report that up to 20% of street-available stimulants currently contain a mixture of both methaphetamine and cocaine (Albertson et al., 1999). To address these phenomena, some studies have utilized a combined group of cocaine and methamphetamine users rather than examining these drug users as separate groups (Ceballos et al., 2005b; Lawton-Craddock et al., 2003).

As early as 1990, cocaine plus alcohol was identified as one of the most commonly abused drug combinations in the United States (Bunney et al., 2001; Grant and Harford, 1990). In fact, the Epidemiological Catchment Area Survey (Reiger et al., 1990), indicated that the association between drug and alcohol dependence was strongest for this group (See Kranzler and Rosenthal, 2003). Approximately 84% of those positive for cocaine abuse/dependence also endorsed an alcohol use disorder (Kranzler and Rosenthal, 2003). Previous surveys have indicated that in addition to significant *concurrent* use of alcohol and cocaine (defined as use within the same month period), *simultaneous* use of these substances is also quite common (Bunney et al., 2001; Grant and Harford, 1990). The frequency of simultaneous use is of particular interest given the generation of pharmacologically active by-products, such as cocaethylene (Bunney et al., 2001; Brookoff et al., 1996; Grant and Harford, 1990). Initial hypotheses suggested that cocaethylene formation might increase the already elevated cerebrovascular impact of cocaine abuse; thus, increasing the potential for development of cocaethylene-related neuropsychological abnormalities (Farre et al., 1993; Higgens et al., 1994; McCance-Katz et al., 1993). Current literature remains contentious with regard to whether the combined effect of chronic cocaine and alcohol use results in a more severe effect on cognitive functioning. A number of studies have suggested that simultaneous use of alcohol and cocaine leads to greater deficits than the use of either substance alone (Bolla et al., 2000; Horner et al., 1997). However, other investigations have failed to duplicate this effect (Ceballos et al., 2005b; Di Sclafani et al., 1998; Easton and Bauer 1997; Lawton-Craddock et al., 2003; Robinson et al., 1999). Clearly, co-morbid use of other substances is an issue that must be addressed in all subsequent studies examining the neuropsychological impact of cocaine use.

Another issue that is relevant to the study of the chronic neuropsychological effects of street drug use is the sensitivity of assessment strategies. Standard neuropsychological assessments may not be sensitive to the subtle cognitive decrements that are often observed in detoxified, abstinence street drug users. Rather than focusing on final performance measures in standard neuropsychological tasks, a number of studies have applied the concept of *cognitive efficiency* (See Nixon et al., 1998). As defined within the component processes model, cognitive efficiency refers to an individual's ability to maintain vigilance toward relevant stimuli while correctly identifying and effectively ignoring irrelevant stimuli within a specified time frame (Nixon and Parsons, 1991). These results have been noted using behavioral tasks such as the computerized efficiency battery (Nixon et al., 1998; Lawton-Craddock et al., 2003), ecologically valid tasks such as the Plant Task (Nixon and Parsons, 1991), and electrophysiological measures such as the N400 (Ceballos et al., 2003a; Nixon et al., 2002) and P300 (Ceballos et al., 2003b) waveforms.

Behaviorally, previous studies have conceptualized cognitive efficiency in terms of speed/accuracy trade offs (Glenn and Parsons, 1991), in which substances abusers typically slow their response time in order to concentrate on performing accurately, a finding which could reflect an adaptive response to years of substance use (Nixon et al., 1998; Sullivan et al., 2002). More recently, this method has been applied to the study of illicit stimulant use. Using a computerized battery of neurocognitive tasks assessing visual-spatial skills, problem solving and abstraction, short-term memory, cognitive flexibility and gross motor speed, Lawton-Craddock and colleagues (2003) calculated an overall cognitive efficiency score, composed of the average ratios of percent correct divided by reaction time for each task. Results indicated that participants with a history of illicit stimulant use (cocaine and/or methamphetamine) were significantly less cognitively efficient than control participants. This assessment strategy will be described in greater detail in the example study that will be presented later in the chapter.

METHAMPHETAMINES

The use of ephedrine and pseudoephedrine as precursor substances in the production of methamphetamine has led to exponential growth of small clandestine labs across the United States, posing a particularly severe problem in rural areas (National Institute on Drug Abuse, 2002; Nordahl et al., 2003). Methamphetamine ingestion targets several neurotransmitter systems, most notably the dopaminergic system, although serotonergic, noradrenergic and gluatmatergic systems are also impacted (Nordahl et al., 2003). Multiple routes of administration have been described. The drug may be ingested, snorted, smoked or injected intravenously (Nordahl et al., 2003). The popularity of various administration methods may pose an experimental problem, as some administration methods may provide unwanted variation. Individuals who endorse injection as their primary route of administration have been shown to differ from other groups with regard to methamphetamine usage patterns as well as medical, criminal and psychological histories (Domier et al., 2000). Obviously, injection drug users are also at higher risk of contracting blood borne infections such as Hepatitis B and HIV.

Methamphetamine differs from other illicit stimulants, such as cocaine or un-substituted amphetamine, with regard to usage patterns and bioavailability. Compared to un-substituted amphetamines, methamphetamine has greater lipid solubility and crosses the blood brain barrier more readily (Nordahl et al., 2003). Unlike cocaine, methamphetamine is typically administered on a nearly daily basis, and usage is evenly spaced throughout the day (Simon et al., 2002b). Methamphetamine also has a longer duration of action: 8-13 hours vs. 1-3 for cocaine (Nordahl et al., 2003). Given these characteristics, it is not surprising that chronic use of methamphetamine has been associated with persistent cognitive decrements.

In the clinical setting, distractibility and deficits of sustained attention have been noted in methamphetamine users; however, scientific literature has been relatively sparse with respect to the specific long-term effects of methamphetamine on human cognition (Nordahl et al., 2003; Salo et al., 2002). This trend is reversing as methamphetamine use becomes a more significant and wide-spread problem. Cognitive performance studies of *current* methamphetamine users report drug-related deficits in memory, manipulation of information, perceptual speed, and performance on the Wisconsin Card Sorting Test (Simon et al., 2000, 2002a). Importantly, the aforementioned studies focused exclusively on users of methamphetamine alone, and excluded individuals with a history of dependence on other substances. Urine screening was used to confirm both recency of methamphetamine use and abstinence from other street drugs. Depending on geographical location, identifying an adequate number of individuals who exclusively use methamphetamine could be challenging, and alternative strategies should be considered.

Other studies suggest that grouping participants based on level of severity of drug dependence may be a more refined method of examining cognitive decrements. McKetin and Mattick (1998) utilized the Severity of Dependence Scale (Gossop et al., 1995) to categorize methamphetamine users based on level of dependence. Using this method, they found that the most dramatic cognitive decrements, in verbal memory, attention/concentration and delayed recall, were observed in participants who were classified as "highly dependent". Interestingly, individuals of "low dependence" did not show significant cognitive impairment.

In the early stages of abstinence (e.g., 5-14 days), methamphetamine dependent individuals perform significantly worse than control subjects on measures of attention/psychomotor speed, verbal learning and memory, and executive system measures sensitive to fluency (Kalechstein et al., 2003). In addition to standard neuropsychological assessments, methamphetamine users with an average of 25 days of abstinence (range 6-46 days), also exhibit cognitive differences relative to control participants on tasks designed to assess decision making processes (Paulus et al., 2003). Salo et al. (2002) reported reduced cognitive inhibition and deficits of explicit attentional performance in detoxified methamphetamine users with 2 to 4 months of abstinence prior to testing. Thus, some cognitive deficits appear to persist even after protracted abstinence, a finding that is supported by reports of decreased brain metabolism in methamphetamine users with long-term abstinence (Wang et al., 2004).

CLUB DRUGS

A relatively recent phenomenon compared to other street drug trends, the chronic neuropsychological effects of "club drugs" such as 3,4-methylenedioxymethamphetamine (MDMA, ecstasy), gama-hydroxy butyric acid (GHB), and ketamine have not been studied extensively. Two of these substances, GBH and ketamine, were originally marketed for use in anesthetic medicine. GHB was eventually discontinued as an anesthetic due to its prolonged and variable duration of action (Gonzalez and Nutt, 2005; Meyer et al., 2005). However, this substance has recently resurfaced as a street drug, often referred to as "liquid ecstasy", which is prized for its euphoric, sedative and anabolic effects (National Institute on Drug Abuse, 2005). Unfortunately, the same characteristics that led to its discontinuation as an anesthetic also contribute to its toxicity as a street drug, and GHB overdose can lead to respiratory depression, coma, seizures and even death (Meyer et al., 2005; National Institute on Drug Abuse, 2005). Chronic use of GHB is associated with severe withdrawal syndrome that includes insomnia, anxiety, tremors and sweating (Meyer et al., 2005; National Institute on Drug Abuse, 2005). Recent studies have identified that individuals intoxicated by GHB exhibit poor performance on field sobriety tests and exhibit confusion, incoherent speech, unresponsiveness, lack of balance, unsteady coordination, and varying states of wakefulness (Couper and Logan, 2001). At this time, little is known about the long-term effects of GHB on cognitive functioning.

Ketamine remains a popular anesthetic for veterinary practice; however, in recent years, ketamine has also gained notoriety as street drug commonly known as "special K" (National Institute on Drug Abuse, 2005; Ricaurte and McCann, 2005). Ketamine intoxication results in dream-like states, but can also lead to delirium, amnesia, impaired motor function, high blood pressure, depression and potentially fatal respiratory problems (NIDA, 2005). The literature is relatively sparse with regard to the effects of acute and chronic ketamine use on cognitive performance. Early reports linked ketamine administration to impaired performance on tests of vigilance, verbal fluency, delayed word recall and the Wisconsin Card Sorting Test (Krystal et al., 1994). More recent investigations by Morgan and colleagues have replicated and extended these findings by testing chronic ketamine users in comparison to poly-drug controls. Three days after ketamine use, chronic ketamine users exhibited persistent impairment on tasks tapping episodic and semantic memory (Morgan et al., 2004b). A 3-year longitudinal follow-up study indicated that episodic, but not semantic, memory deficits may persist even after marked reduction of ketamine use (Morgan et al., 2004a).

Because MDMA has been the most extensively researched with regard to cognitive effects, this remainder of this section will focus on the literature pertaining to this drug. Early case studies suggested that MDMA might lead to increased psychiatric symptomatology (McGuire, 2000). As noted previously, studies involving users of any street drug should carefully assess psychiatric co-morbidity and account for these issues in statistical analyses if it is not possible to address this issue in experimental design. However, as with other street drugs, it is important to consider that individuals with pre-morbid psychiatric symptomatology may be more inclined to initiate drug use (Kranzler and Rosenthal, 2003). This notion is supported by the work of McGuire and colleagues (1994), who found that among a sample of MDMA users with psychiatric concerns, 50% endorsed a history of transient psychiatric symptoms unrelated to MDMA use, and 50% also reported a first degree relative with psychiatric illness (McGuire, 2000). Further, a number of pre-morbid psychiatric and psychological conditions, including personality disorders, may mimic deficits observed in street drug users (Bauer, 2001a; Costa and Bauer, 1998; Stevens et al., 2001).

Acute doses of MDMA primarily lead to increases in serotonin and dopamine, although other neurotransmitters such as norepinephrine, acetylcholine and histamine are affected as well (Parrott, 2004). MDMA has been described as a serotonergic neurotoxin (Gouzoulis-Mayfrank et al., 2005; Ricaurte et al., 2000). These effects correspond to a growing literature that reports persistent decrements in learning and memory, as well as short-term or working memory, among human MDMA users (See Gouzoulis-Mayfrank et al., 2005). Even among abstinent MDMA users, these effects have been observed in a variety of studies employing different neuropsychological testing techniques, control groups, and degrees of abstinence (Back-Madruga et al., 2003; Bhattachary and Powell, 2001; Bolla et al., 1998; Gouzoulis-Mayfrank et al., 2000, 2003, 2005; Hanson and Luciana, 2004; Krystal and Price, 1992; McCardle et al., 2004; Parrot et al., 1998; Parrot and Lasky, 1998; Reneman et al., 2000; Rodgers, 2001; Rodgers et al., 2003; Wareing et al., 2004; Verkes et al., 2001; Zakzanis and Young, 2001). In addition to the commonly noted working memory deficit, MDMA may also have an adverse effect on analogical reasoning in detoxified, abstinent users (Verdejo-Garcia et al., 2005).

As with other street drug research in human populations, the MDMA literature is plagued with a number of methodological issues. Of particular importance to the study of "designer drugs" such MDMA, are issues related to uncertain dosage and the purity and chemical composition of illegally purchased substances (Curran, 2000; Gouzoulis-Mayfrank et al., 2005). Obviously, such variation may be difficult to control in studies of human street drug users. Another issue to be considered is that MDMA users frequently report the routine use of more than one substance (Halpern et al., 2004). Recent studies have identified a differential profile of neuropsychological deficits associated with use of MDMA, cocaine and marijuana (Verdejo-Garcia et al., 2005); thus, the potential contributions of these substances to neuropsychological deficits are far from trivial. As much as possible, experimental designs must account for the potential influences of other chronic or acute drug use on cognitive functioning. To address this concern, studies have employed a variety of approaches from strict recruitment criteria limiting the substance abuse history of participants (Halpern et al., 2004) to enforced abstinence from various drugs prior to testing (Gouzoulis-Mayfrank et al., 2005). Other authors have employed statistical adjustment to account for levels of non-MDMA drug use (Fox et al., 2001, 2002; Halpern et al., 2004; Heffernan et al., 2001; Reneman et al., 2001; Verkes et al., 2001; Wareing et al., 2000).

Finally, longitudinal assessment is a particularly important approach when examining the effects of relatively understudied street drugs. This approach may be used to address the question of whether or not cognitive recovery is possible with continued abstinence. Recent data suggest that MDMA-related deficits may persist following prolonged abstinence. For instance, despite a significant drop-out rate of approximately 63%, Gouzoulis-Mayfrank and colleagues (2005) observed that individuals who maintained abstinence from MDMA over an 18 month follow-up period failed to exhibit significant recovery of memory decrements.

PRESCRIPTION DRUGS

Abuse and dependence upon prescription drugs is a major problem in the United States. Many classes of prescription drugs are subject to abuse/dependence including stimulants (e.g., methylphenidate), sedatives and tranquilizers (e.g., barbiturates, benzodiazepines) and opioid analgesics (e.g., oxycontin, hydrocodone) (National Institute on Drug Abuse, 2001). However, in the 2003 National Household Survey on Drug Abuse, 4.7 million individuals endorsed misuse of analgesic medications, making them the most widely abused of prescription psychoactive medications (Isaacson et al., 2005). In fact, the number of analgesic users was more than twice that of the next most frequently abused drug class, tranquilizers (1.8 million users). The Drug Abuse Warning Network (DAWN) estimates that emergency room visits resulting from opioid analgesic abuse have been increasing since 1994 (United States Department of Health and Human Services, 2002). Specifically, oxycodone and hydrocodone were most frequently noted, accounting for 40% of all opioid-related visits.

When planning studies of prescription drug use, a number of demographic issues should be recognized. First, prescription drug abuse has been associated with both younger age, and a lifetime history of illicit substance use (Isaacson et al., 2005; Reid et al., 2002). Interestingly, a recent study by Potter et al., (2004) indicates that individuals who abuse oxycodone are likely to have a history of substance abuse, regardless of whether analgesics were obtained illicitly or via legitimate pain complaint. Secondly, in the United States, women are nearly 50% more likely than men to be prescribed a controlled substance (Isaacson et al., 2005; Simoni-Wastila, 2000). However, abuse-related gender effects are lacking, with the exception of the 12-17 year age group, in which females are more likely than males to abuse prescription substances (National Institute on Drug Abuse, 2005).

Oxycodone acts on mu-opioid receptors to produce a mild sense of euphoria, consequently providing effective pain relief (Stahl, 2000; Zacny and Gutierrez, 2003). Surprisingly, although oxycodone has been in clinical use since 1915, the basic pharmacology of this drug has been a neglected field of research (Kalso, 2005; Zacny and Gutierrez, 2003). For instance, the metabolism of oxycodone in humans is still poorly characterized, although recent studies suggest that a great deal of inter-individual variability exists (Kalso, 2005; Lugo and Kern, 2004). Research has supported the idea that oxycodone is as dangerous as other opiates and can be lethal if abused (Drummer, et al., 1994). Fatalities from oxycodone abuse alone have been noted, but combined drug toxicity with a benzodiazepine is most commonly observed (Wolf et al., 2005). In general, side effects of opiate analgesics include sedation, respiratory depression, decrements of attentional function, poor perception of spatial relations and decreased motor skills, particularly hand-eye coordination (Allen et al., 2003; Bradley and Nicholson, 1986).

Acutely, hydrocodone administration has been associated with performance deficits on simple tracking and reaction time tasks (Allen et al., 2003).

Although the literature is sparse with respect to the long-term effects of prescription analgesic abuse on cognition, previous studies of chronic opiate use suggest that prior use of these drugs should be an important consideration in the design of studies of street drug using populations. It is important to note that studies summarized in this section refer to drug *abuse*, rather than merely the occasional or recreational use of prescription substances. Davis and colleagues (2002) reported that 60% of current opioid abusers demonstrated cognitive impairments of at least two standard deviations below norms on two or more neuropsychological tests, thereby indicating a significant difference when compared with the control group. Their findings suggested that neuropsychological deficits are increased in opiate abusers, but recovery may likely occur over time with abstinence. For instance, Verdejo and colleagues (2005) sought to assess potential neuropsychological deficits demonstrated by current opioid users compared to a group of previous opioid users who were currently abstinent. They found significantly worse performance by current opioid users on tests of processing speed, visuo-spatial attention, and cognitive flexibility. Results also indicated that current users were less accurate on working memory and analogical reasoning tests.

SUMMARY

Although a full review of street drug literature is beyond the scope of this chapter, the foregoing tutorial highlighted a number of issues that have historically complicated studies of neuropsychological function in this population. Issues include the concurrent use of multiple substances both legal and illegal, variability in drug composition and potency, level of abstinence, detection of relapse, appropriateness of comparison groups, sensitivity of assessment strategies, severity of drug use or dependence, presence of pre- or co-morbid psychiatric symptomatology, and other demographic information.

Various approaches to dealing with experimental obstacles were presented from the current street drug literature as a means of illustrating the importance of these issues. Like all clinical research, studies in street drug using populations are quasi-experimental, producing correlational data rather than giving an indication of true cause and effect (Rogers and Robbins, 2001). For this reason, studies must be designed careful to control, as much as possible, the myriad sources of variation that occur in street drug using populations.

**Table 1. Issues of Concern in the Scientific Investigation
of Cognitive Decrements in Street Drug Users**

Use of Multiple Illicit and Licit Drugs
Variability in Drug Composition and Potency
Level of Abstinence
Detection of Relapse
Appropriateness of Comparison Group
Sensitivity of Assessment Strategy
Severity of Drug Use or Dependence
Psychiatric Symptomatology
Demographics

EXAMPLE STUDY

The following research study utilized a computerized, visual continuous performance test (CPT) to examine sustained attention in detoxified, abstinent street drug abusers (SD), alcoholics (ALC), community controls (CTRL) without a significant history of alcohol or drug dependence. Participants were recruited from the treatment setting, and had attained a level of abstinence / sobriety ranging from 21 to 45 days. It is clinically important to understand the nature of cognitive efficiency deficits that may occur during this early abstinence period, as even subtle decrements could affect patients' ability to respond to the myriad of stimuli presented during the treatment experience. Of particular interest is how chronic use of alcohol alone, or in combination with street drugs, affects vigilance (i.e., sustained attention).

In accordance with studies mentioned previously in the chapter, rather than focusing on end-point performance, the authors applied a process-oriented approach, which focused on cognitive efficiency as defined within the component processes model. Based on previous reports of attentional decrements in alcoholics and street drug users (Beatty et al., 1995; Simon et al., 2002a; Tedstone and Coyle, 2004), the authors hypothesized that the patient groups would exhibit poorer performance relative to controls, with street drug abusers exhibiting the poorest cognitive efficiency (Lawton-Craddock et al., 2003; Nixon et al., 1998). Given previous work (Ceballos et al., 2003a; Nixon and Bowlby, 1996; Nixon and Parsons, 1991; Nixon et al., 1998; Nixon et al., 2002), it was predicted that these decrements would appear as a subtle decrease in cognitive efficiency rather than an overt deficit in accuracy or response time.

STUDY METHODS

Participants

The Institutional Review Board of the University of Oklahoma Health Sciences Center approved all phases of study, and written informed consent was obtained prior to participation in the study. One hundred eighty-six participants were tested. Sixty-three street drug abusers (45 male; SD) and 58 detoxified alcoholics (35 male; ALC) were recruited from local substance abuse treatment centers including state, federal, and privately operated facilities.

All patient groups had obtained between 21 and 45 days of sobriety/ abstinence prior to neurocognitive testing. Individuals included in the ALC group met DSM-III-R (American Psychiatric Association (APA), 1987) and/or DSM-IV (American Psychiatric Association, 1994) criteria for alcohol abuse or dependence as determined by chart review and structured interview (Diagnostic Interview Schedule, Version IV (DIS-IV); Robbins et al., 1995). In addition to meeting criteria for inclusion within the ALC group, individuals included in the SD group simultaneously met diagnostic criteria for abuse or dependence upon one or more street drugs. Data collection extended across DSM-III-R and DSM-IV.

Sixty-five community controls (33 male; CTRL) were recruited using newspaper ads, flyers and word-of-mouth. To be included within the control group, participants were required to have no history of substance abuse treatment or a regular drinking pattern of more than three drinks per occasion over the 6 months prior to testing. Regardless of group classification, all participants were screened for current or previous neurological, medical, or psychiatric conditions expected to affect cognition.

Background Variables

A number of background measures were collected as part of a larger, ongoing study. In additional to general demographic information, other measures included depressive symptomatology (Beck Depression Inventory

(BDI); Beck et al., 1996), state anxiety (Spielberger State Anxiety Inventory (SSAI); Spielberger, 1983), and verbal and abstracting skill (Shipley Institute of Living Scale-Revised (SVAGE, SAAGE); Zachary, 1986). To characterize the drinking patterns of participants, a quantity frequency index (QFI; Cahalan et al., 1969), representing the average number of ounces of absolute ethanol consumed per day over the 6 months prior to testing, was also administered.

Continuous Performance Test

The current study utilized a computerized "FTK" version of the CPT adapted from ForThought, Ltd. (Nashua, NH). During the task subjects in each group were presented a series of pseudo-random letters on a computer screen and instructed to respond, via a push button response pad, to a specific target combination ("FTK"). The CPT was administered to each subject individually in a quiet room with the lights dimmed. Before testing began, interactive instructions were provided to assure understanding of the procedure. Stimuli were presented in four presentation blocks. Dependent variables were recorded separately for each presentation block and included number of responses, number of correct responses, omission and commission errors, and response time.

Data Analysis

Statistical analyses were performed using SPSS Version 11.0 for Windows. Background variables were examined using factorial analyses of variance (ANOVAs). CPT variables were analyzed via 3 (group) X (4 presentation period) ANOVAs with repeated presentation blocks. Greenhouse-Geisser corrections were applied to within-subjects effects to guard against violations of the sphericity assumption. In all analyses, significant differences were followed by pair-wise comparisons of estimated marginal means. Significant group differences on demographic variables expected to confound interpretation of CPT variables were further examined using correlational analyses with a significance level of $p < .001$ to control Type 1 error associated with the large number of tests. In all analyses, ns of less than 186 indicate missing data.

Study Results

Background Variables

Results are summarized in Table 1. Participants were approximately 73% Caucasian, 21% African American, <1% Hispanic, 4% American Indian and 1% Other. Gender was equally distributed across groups. Group differences in age were observed ($F(2,183)=3.75$, $p=.03$). The SD group was significantly younger than both the ALC and CTRL groups ($p \leq .04$), which did not differ significantly from one another. However, it is important to note that mean age, although significantly different in a statistical sense, was within the same decade across groups. Education also differed across groups ($F(2,183)=10.80$, $p<.001$). The SD group reported significantly fewer years of education than other groups ($ps \leq .005$), which reported statistically similar levels of education. However, as in the case of age, it is important to consider not only the statistical, but the practical, significance of these mean differences. Verbal performance differed across groups ($F(2,180)=19.58$, $p<.001$), and all groups differed significantly from one another ($ps \leq .004$). Controls exhibited the highest verbal score, whereas the SD group exhibited the poorest performance.

Group differences were also noted for abstraction scores ($F(2,177)=12.37$, $p<.001$), and all groups differed from one another on this measure ($ps \leq .04$). Controls exhibited the highest scores; whereas, the SD group performed most poorly. Groups also differed on depressive symptomatology ($F(2,180)=21.34$, $p<.001$). Both patient groups higher BDI-II scores compared to the control group ($ps<.001$). Similarly, groups differed on state anxiety ($F(2,182)=9.35$, $p<.001$). Controls exhibited a lower level of anxiety compared to ALC and SD groups ($ps \leq .03$), which did not differ statistically from one another. However, it is important to note that levels of depression and anxiety were not clinically significant. As expected, a significant group effect was noted for QFI ($F(2,183)=42.71$, $p<.001$). The control group's QFI was significantly lower than both patient groups ($ps<.001$), although ALC and SD groups did not differ significantly from one another. The ALC and SD groups were also statistically similar with respect to chronicity of problem drinking.

Correlations were performed to determine if statistical group differences in depressive symptomatology, state anxiety, age and years of education were likely to confound interpretation of the dependent variables of interest. Results failed to indicate a highly significant pattern of correlations across measures. Thus, due to the lack of compelling evidence of a potential confound, these variables were excluded from subsequent analyses.

**Table 2. Background Variables for Controls, Alcoholics and Street Drug
Abusers, Estimated Marginal Means (Standard Error)**

	Controls (n=65)	Alcoholics (n=58)	Street Drug Abusers (n=63)
% Male	51%	60%	71%
Age*	37.1 (0.9)a	38.0 (1.0)a	34.4 (1.0)b
Education*	13.5 (0.2)a	13.0 (0.2)a	12.2 (0.2)b
SILS-V*	17.9 (0.2)a	17.0 (0.2)b	16.0 (0.2)c
SILS-A*	16.5 (0.3)a	15.5 (0.4)b	14.2 (0.3)b
BDI*	2.0 (0.6)b	6.8 (0.7)a	7.5 (0.7)a
SSAI*	44.1 (1.2)b	47.9 (1.2)a	51.1 (1.2)a
QFI*	0.2 (1.1)c	13.6 (1.1)a	11.3 (1.1)a

*Significant group difference (p<.05). SILS-V = Shipley Institute of Living Scale –
Verbal Age; SILS-A = Shipley Institute of Living Scale – Abstraction Age; BDI =
Beck Depression Inventory; SSAI = Spielberger State Anxiety Index; QFI =
Quantity Frequency Index of Alcohol Consumption.

CPT Variables

Differences in number of correct responses, reaction time and errors of
ommission by group, presentation block and their interaction term were non-
significant. Similarly, group and interactive differences were also non-
significant for errors of commission, although a significant effect of
presentation block was observed ($F(2.86,522.78)=16.32$, $p<.001$), in which the
overall number of errors decreased with each successive block. Subsequent
analyses indicated that all presentation blocks differed significantly from one
another ($ps\leq.03$), with the exception of blocks 3 vs. 4.

However, it is interesting to note that a group X presentation block
interaction was noted with regard to total number of responses
($F(5.72,523.12)=3.30$, $p=.004$). This effect is summarized in Figure 1. The
control group demonstrated increased cognitive efficiency over time by
reducing the number of responses in each successive presentation block, while
maintaining a relatively constant level of correct responding. Patient groups
appeared to employ alternate strategies, as evidence by differences in number
of responses relative to controls.

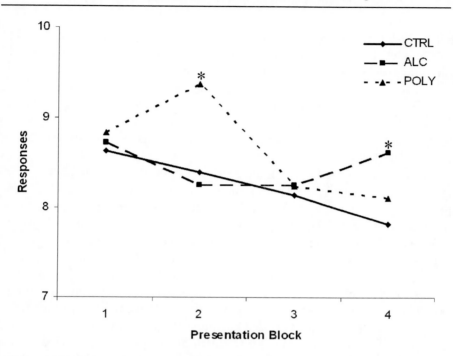

Figure 1. Group Response Rate by Presentation Block. In this Figure, the term POLY refers to the SD group. Although groups did not differ with respect to correct responses or overall accuracy, an interactive effect of group and presentation block was noted for total number of responses [$F(5.72,523.12)=3.30$, $p=.004$]. The efficiency of the CTRL group appeared to increase over time, as evidenced by a decrease in the number of responses in each successive presentation block. Patient groups failed to exhibit this pattern, and group differences were observed for SD vs. other groups in block 2 ($ps \leq .009$) and ALC vs. CTRL in block 4 ($p<.05$).

These group differences reached statistical significance in presentation block 2 ($F(2,183)=5.30$; $p=.006$), in which the SD group exhibited a greater number of responses compared to other groups ($ps \leq .009$). A notable trend also occurred in presentation block 4 ($F(2,183)=2.05$; $p=.13$), and pair-wise comparison revealed a increased responding in the ALC group relative to controls ($p<.05$).

Study Discussion

Although some exceptions have been noted (Damos and Parker, 1994), previous studies have failed to detect chronic alcohol or substance abuse-related differences in performance on sustained attention tasks (Bauer, 2001b; Fallgatter et al., 1998). However, rather than focusing on standard measures of end-point performance, the present study utilized a component processes approach to examine cognitive efficiency of sustained attention. The component processes approach has successfully been applied to examine chronic alcohol and substance abuse-related deficits in a variety of contexts (Ceballos et al., 2003a; Nixon and Bowlby, 1996; Nixon and Parsons, 1991; Nixon et al., 1998).

In the current study, our findings demonstrate that patient groups may employ a less organized response strategy to arrive at the same end-point performance as controls. Although these differences in response strategy are most apparent in presentation periods 2 and 4, the lack of significant group differences in presentation period 3 is also meaningful. This performance pattern clearly suggests a failure to *sustain* cognitive efficiency over time. For instance, despite some periods of equivalent performance, both street drug abusers and alcoholics failed to exhibit a pattern of increasing cognitive efficiency over time as seen in the control group. These results are consistent with previous findings of decreased cognitive efficiency in substance abusing populations (Ceballos et al., 2003a; Nixon and Bowlby, 1996; Nixon and Parsons, 1991; Nixon et al., 1998). Given these preliminary findings, future investigations designed to determine performance patterns beyond the current number of presentation periods are warranted.

In addition, the differential response strategy of the SD group in relation to controls confirmed our initial hypotheses that the combined use of multiple substances may have a more detrimental effect on cognitive function relative to the use of alcohol alone. However, it is important to note that the response strategy of the ALC group also differed from controls, albeit in a less statistically significant manner. The current study is limited by the conglomeration of street drug abusers into one experimental group. Additional work, focusing on the separate and combined effect of licit and illicit substances on cognitive efficiency is warranted. Such attempts to disentangle the separate and interactive effects of multiple substances are particularly timely given the recent rise in polysubstance use among treatment-seeking patients (Substance Abuse and Mental Health Services Administration, 2000). Knowledge gained from such research enhances our understanding of subtle decrements that may be present during the early phases of substance abuse treatment. This information may be applied to improve treatment outcome.

STUDY CONCLUSION

Patients with a history of alcohol dependence and/or street drug use may exhibit subtle decrements of cognitive efficiency. In the current study, patient groups exhibited an inability to maintain or improve cognitive efficiency over time in response to a sustained attention task. These results extend previous reports of cognitive inefficiency in patients with alcohol dependence alone or in combination with illicit drugs. Such attempts to disentangle the contributions of these substances to cognitive efficiency deficits enhance both basic and clinical knowledge.

CHAPTER CONCLUSION

This chapter has focused on issues of relevance to the study of cognitive functioning in chronic street drug users. A number of issues of concern have been identified, which partially account for the paucity of research in this arena. Although this chapter was not designed as an all inclusive review of the street drug literature, it is clear that patients with a history of street drug use exhibit subtle decrements of cognitive performance, which may or may not resolve over time.

Current literature acknowledges that cognitive deficits in street drug users may interfere directly with recovery programs, in both the course of treatment and its results (Rogers and Robbins, 2001; Verdejo-Garcia, 2005). In particular, decrements of memory and attentional functioning may interfere with didactic components of the treatment protocol (Rogers and Robbins, 2001). In addition, patients may find it difficult to comprehend and assimilate information that is provided in the substance abuse treatment setting, to plan behaviors based on objectives that do not involve an immediate reward, and to inhibit inappropriate impulsive responses (Verdejo-Garcia et al., 2005). Depending on patterns of street drug use, and level of pre- or co-morbid psychiatric symptomatology, some street drug users may recover or improve their cognitive functioning with continued abstinence. Treatment programs may improve their effectiveness by adapting to the time constraints of recovery of cognitive function, and by incorporating these aspects into the therapeutic process (Verdejo-Garcia et al., 2005).

AUTHOR NOTE

This work was supported in part by NIAAA RO1-AA09163 (S.J.N, PI). Data presented in the example study were collected in the Cognitive Studies Laboratory, directed by S.J.N. at the University of Oklahoma Health Sciences Center. The authors wish to extend special thanks to the former research assistants, consultants and staff of the Cognitive Studies Laboratory.

REFERENCES

Albertson, T.E., Derlet, R.W., and Van Hoozen, B.E. (1999). Methamphetamine and the expanding complications of amphetamines. *Western Journal of Medicine, 170,* 214-219.

Allen, G.J., Hartl, T.L., Duffany, S., Smith, S.F., Van Heest, J.L., Anderson, J.M., Hoffman, J.R., Kraemer, W.L., and Maresh, C.M. (2003). Cognitive and motor function after administration of hydrocodone bitartrate plus ibuprofen, ibuprofen alone, or placebo in healthy subjects with exercise-induced muscle damage: A randomized, repeated-dose, placebo-controlled study. *Psychopharmacology, 166,* 228-233.

American Psychiatric Association. (1987*). Diagnostic and Statistical Manual of Mental Disorders, 3rd Edition – Revised.* Washington, D.C.: American Psychiatric Press.

American Psychiatric Association. (1994). *Diagnostic and Statistical Manual of Mental Disorders, 4th Edition.* Washington, D.C.: American Psychiatric Association.

Back-Madruga, C., Boone, K.B., Chang, L., Grab, C.S., Lee, A., Nations, H., and Poland, R.E. (2003). Neuropsychological effects of 3,4-methylenedioxymethamphetamine (MDMA or ecstasy) in recreational users. *Clinical Neuropsychology, 17,* 446-459.

Bhattachary, S., and Powell, J.H. (2001). Recreational use of 3,4-methylenedioxymethamphetamine (MDMA) or "ecstasy": Evidence for cognitive impairment. *Psychological Medicine, 31,* 647-658.

Bauer, L.O. (2001a). Antisocial personality disorder and cocaine dependence: their effects on behavioral and electroencephalographic measures of time estimation. *Drug Alcohol Dependence, 63,* 87-95.

Bauer, L.O. (2001b). CNS recovery from cocaine, cocaine and alcohol, or opioid dependence: A P300 study. *Clinical Neurophysiology, 112,* 1508-1515.

Beck, A., Steer, R.A., and Garbin, M.G. (1988). Psychometric properties of the Beck Depression Inventory: Twenty-five years of evaluation. *Clinical Psychology Review, 8,* 77-100.

Beatty, W.W., Katzung, V.M., Moreland, V.J., and Nixon, S.J. (1995). Neuropsychological performance of recently abstinent alcoholics and cocaine abusers. *Drug and Alcohol Dependence, 37,* 247-253.

Berry, J., van Gorp, W., Herzberg, D.S., Hinkin, C., Boone, K., Steinman, L., and Wilkins, J.N. (1993). Neuropsychological deficits in abstinent cocaine abusers: preliminary findings after two weeks of abstinence. *Drug and Alcohol Dependence, 32,* 231-237.

Bolla, K.I., Funderburk, F.R., and Cadet, J.L. (2000). Differential effects of cocaine and cocaine + alcohol on neurocognitive performance. *Neurology, 54,* 2285-2292.

Bolla, K., McCann, U., and Ricaurte, G. (1998). Imparied memory function in abstinent 3,4-methylenedioxymethamphetamine (MDMA, 'ecstasty') users. *Neurology, 51,* 1532-1537.

Bradley, C.M., and Nicholson, A.N. (1986). Effects of a mu-opioid receptor agonist (codeine phosphate) on visuo-motor coordination and dynamic visual acuity in man. *British Journal of Clinical Pharmacology, 22,* 507-512.

Brookoff, D., Rotondo, M.F., Shaw, L.M., Campbell, E.A., and Fields, L. (1996). Cocaethylene levels in patients who test positive for cocaine. *Annals of Emergency Medicine, 27,* 316-320.

Bunney, E.B., Appel, S.B., and Brodie, M.S. (2001). Electrophysiological effects of cocaethylene, cocaine, and ethanol on dopaminergic neurons of the ventral tegmental area. *The Journal of Pharmacology and Experimental Therapeutics, 297,* 696-703.

Cahalan, D., Cissin, I.H., and Crossley, H.M. (1969). *American Drinking Practices: A National Study of Drinking Behavior and Attitudes.* New Brunswick, NJ: Rutgers Center of Alcohol Studies.

Ceballos, N.A., Nixon, S.J., Phillips, J.A., and Tivis, R.D. (2003a). Semantic processing in alcoholics with and without antisocial symptomatology. *Journal of Studies on Alcohol, 64,* 286-291.

Ceballos, N.A., Nixon, S.J., and Tivis, R.D. (2003b). Substance abuse-related P300 differences in response to an implicit memory task. *Progress in Neuro-Psychopharmacology and Biological Psychiatry, 27,* 157-164.

Ceballos, N.A., Houston, R.J., Smith, N.D., Bauer, L.O., and Taylor, R.E. (2005a). N400 as an index of semantic expectancies: Differential effects of alcohol and cocaine dependence. *Progress in Neuropsychopharmacology and Biological Psychiatry, 29*, 936-943.

Ceballos, N.A., Tivis, R., Lawton-Craddock, A., and Nixon, S.J. (2005b). Visual-spatial attention in alcoholics and illicit stimulant abusers: Effects of nicotine replacement. *Progress in Neuropsychopharmacology and Biological Psychiatry, 29*, 97-107.

Childers, S.R., and Breivogel, C.S. (1998). Cannabis and endogeous cannabinoid systems. *Drug and Alcohol Dependence, 51*, 173-187.

Corey, S. (2005). Recent developments in the therapeutic potential of cannabinoids. *Puerto Rico Health Sciences Journal, 24*, 19-26.

Cornish, J.W., and O'Brien, C.P. (1996). Crack cocaine abuse: an epidemic with many public health consequences. *Annual Review of Public Health, 17*, 259-273.

Costa, L., and Bauer, L.O. (1998). Smooth pursuit eye movement dysfunction in substance-dependent patients: mediating effects of antisocial personality disorder. *Neuropsychobiology, 37*, 117-23.

Costa e Silva, J.A. (2002). Evidence-based analysis of the worldwide abuse of licit and illicit drugs. *Human Psychopharmacology, 17*, 131-140.

Couper, F.J., and Logan, B.K. (2001). GHB and driving impairment. *Journal of Forensic Science., 46*, 919-923.

Curran, V.H. (2000). Is MDMA (ecstasy) neurotoxic in humans? An overview of evidence and of methodological problems in research. *Neuropsychobiology, 42*, 34-41.

Di Sclafani, V., Clark, H., Tolou-Shams, M., Bloomer, C.W., Salas, G.A., Norman, D., and Fein, G. (1998). Premorbid brain size is a determinant of functional reserve in abstinent crack-cocaine and crack-cocaine-alcohol-dependent adults. *Journal of the International Neuropsychological Society, 4*, 559-565.

Davis, P.E., Liddiard, H., and McMillan, T.M. (2002). Neuropsychological deficits and opiate abuse. *Drug and Alcohol Dependence, 67*, 105-108.

Domier, C.P., Simon, S.L., Rawson, R.A., Huber, A., and Ling, W. (2000). A comparison of injecting and noninjecting methamphetamine users. *Journal of Psychoactive Drugs, 32*, 229-232.

Drummer, O. H., Syrjanen, M. L., Phelan, M., and Cordner, S. M. (1994). A study of deaths involving oxycodone. *Journal of Forensic Sciences, 39*, 1069-1075.

Easton, C., and Bauer, L.O. (1997). Neuropsychological differences between alcohol-dependent and cocaine-dependent patients with or without problematic drinking.

Psychiatry Research, 71, 97-103.

Elphick, M.R., and Egertova, M. (2001). The neurobiology and evolution of cannabinoid signaling. *Philosophical Transactions of the Royal Society of London. Series B: Biological Sciences, 356,* 381-408.

Fallgatter, A. J., Wiesbeck, G. A., Weijers, H. G., Boening, J., and Strik, *W. K.* (1998).

Event-related correlates of response suppression as indicators of novelty seeking in alcoholics. *Alcohol and Alcoholism, 33,* 475-481.

Farre, M., De la Torre, R., Llorente, M., Lamas, X., Ugena, B., Segura, J., and Cami, J. (1993). Alcohol and cocaine interactions in humans. *Archives of General Psychiatry, 33,* 983-989.

Fox, H.C., Toplis, A.S., Turner, J.J.D., and Parrott, A.C. (2001). Auditory verbal learning in drug-free polydrug users. *Human Psychopharmacology: Clinical and Experimental, 16,* 613-618.

Fox, H.C., McLean, A., Turner, J.J.D., Parrott, A.C., Rogers, R., and Sahakian, B.J. (2002). Neuropsychological evidence of a relatively selective profile of temporal dysfunction in drug-free MDMA ("ecstasy") polydrug users. *Psychopharmacology (Berlin), 162,* 203-214.

Glenn, S.W., and Parsons, O.A. (1991). Effects of alcoholism and instructional conditions on speed/accuracy tradeoffs. *Alcoholism: Clinical and Experimental Research, 15,* 612-619.

Gonzalez, M.S., Carey, C., and Grant, I. (2002). Nonacute (residual) neuropsychological effects of cannabis use: a qualitative analysis and systematic review. *Journal of Clinical Pharmacology, 32,* 48S-57S.

Gonzalez, A., and Nutt, D.J. (2005). Gamma hydroxyl butyrate abuse and dependencey. *Journal of Psychopharmacology, 19,* 195-204.

Gossop, M., Darke, S., Griffiths, P., Hando, J., Powis, B., Hall, W., and Strang, J. (1995). The severity of dependence scale (SDS): Psychometric properties of the SDS in English and Australian samples of heroin, cocaine and amphetamine users. *Addiction, 90,* 607-614.

Gouzoulis-Mayfrank, E., Daumann, J., Tuchtenhagen, F., Pelz, S., Becker, S., Kunert, H-J., Fimm, B., and Sass, H. (2000). Impaired cognitive performance in drug-free recreational ecstasy (MDMA) users. *Journal of Neurology, Neurosurgery and Psychiatry, 68,* 719-725.

Gouzoulis-Mayfrank, E., Fischermann, T., Rezk, M., Thimm, B., Hensen, G., and Daumann, J. (2005). Memory performance in polyvalent MDMA (ecstasy) users who continue or discontinue MDMA use. *Drug and Alcohol Dependence, 78,* 317-323.

Gouzoulis-Mayfrank, E., Thimm, B., Rezk, M., Hensen, G., and Daumann, J. (2003). Memory impairment suggests hippocampi dysfunction in abstinent ecstasy (MDMA) users. *Progress in Neuro-Psychopharmacology and Biological Psychiatry, 27,* 819-827.

Grant, B.F., and Harford, T.C. (1990). Concurrent and simultaneous use of alcohol with cocaine: results of national survey. *Drug and Alcohol Dependence, 25,* 97-104.

Green, B., Kavanagh, D., and Young, R. (2003). Being stoned: A review of self-reported cannabis effects. *Drug and Alcohol Review, 22,* 453-460.

Hall, W., and Swift, W. (2000). The THC content of cannabis in Australia: Evidence and implications. *Australian and New Zealand Journal of Public Health, 24,* 503-508.

Halpern, H., Pope, H.G. Jr., Sherwood, A.R., Barry, S., Hudson, J.I., and Yurgelun-Todd, D. (2004). Residual neuropsychological effects of illicit 3,4-methylenedioxymethamphetamine (MDMA) in individuals with minimal exposure to other drugs. *Drug and Alcohol Dependence, 75,* 135-147.

Hanson, K.L., and Luciana, M. (2004). Neurocognitive function in users of MDMA: the importance of clinically significant patterns of use. *Psychological Medicine, 34,* 229-246.

Heffernan, T.M., Jarvis, H., Rodgers, J., Scholey, A.B., and Ling, J. (2001). Prospective memory, everday cognitive failure and central executive function in recreational users of Ecstasy. *Human Psychopharmacology, 16,* 607-612.

Higgins, S.T., Budney, A.J., Bickel, W.K., Foerg, F.E., and Badger, G.J. (1994). Alcohol dependence and alcohol use in cocaine-dependent patients. *Journal of Addictive Disorders, 13,* 177-189.

Horner, M.D. (1997). Cognitive functioning in alcoholic patients with and without cocaine dependence. *Archives of Clinical Neuropsychology, 12,* 667-676.

Huestis, M.A., and Cone, E.J. (1998). Differentiating new marijuana use from residual drug excretion in occasional marijuana users. *Journal of Analytical Toxicology, 22,* 445-454.

Isaacson, H.J., Hopper, J.A., Alford, D.P., and Parran, T. (2005). Prescription drug use and abuse. *Postgraduate Medicine, 118,* 19-26.

Kalechstein, A.D., Newton, T.F., and Green, M. (2003). Methamphetamine dependence is associated with neurocognitive impairment in the initial phases of abstinence. *Journal of Neuropsychiatry and Clinical Neuroscience, 15,* 215-220.

Kalso, E. (2005). Oxycodone. *Journal of Pain and Symptom Management, 29,* S47-S56.

Kranzler, H.R., and Rosenthal, R.N. (2003). Dual diagnosis: Alcoholism and co-morbid psychiatric disorders. *The American Journal on Addictions, 12 (Suppl 1),* S26-S40.

Krystal, J.H., Karper, L.P., Seibyl, J.P., Freeman, G.K., Delaney, R., Bremner, J.D., Heninger, G.R., Bowers, M.B. Jr., and Charney, D.S. (1994). Subanesthetic effects of the noncompetitive NMDA antagonist, Ketamine, in humans. Psychotomimetic, perceptual, cognitive and neuroendocrine responses. *Archives of General Psychiatry, 51,* 199-214.

Krystal, J., and Price, L. (1992). Chronic 3,4-methylene-dioxy-methamphetamine (MDMA) use: effects on mood and neuropsychological function? *American Journal of Drug and Alcohol Abuse, 18,* 331-334.

Lawton-Craddock, A., Nixon, S.J., and Tivis, R. (2003). Cognitive efficiency in stimulant abusers with and without alcohol dependence. *Alcoholism: Clinical and Experimental Research, 27,* 457-64.

Lugo, R.A., and Kern, S.E. (2004). The pharmacokinetics of oxycodone. *Journal of Pain and Palliative Care Pharmacotherapy, 28,* 17-30.

Lyketsos, C.G., Garrett, E., Liang, K.Y., and Anthony, J.C. (1999). Cannabis use and cognitive decline in persons under 65 years of age. *American Journal of Epidemiology, 149,* 794-800.

McCance-Katz, E.F., Price, L.H., McDougle, C.J., Kosten, T.R., Black, J.E., and Jatlow, P.I. (1993). Concurrent cocaine-ethanol ingestion in humans: Pharmacology, physiology, behavior and the role of cocaethylene. *Psychopharmacology, 111,* 39-46.

McCardle, K., Luebbers, S., Carter, J.D., Croft, R.J., and Stough, C. (2004). Chronic MDMA (ecstasy) use, cognition and mood. *Psychopharmacology, 173,* 434-439.

McGuire, P. (2000). Long term psychiatric and cognitive effects of MDMA use. *Toxicology Letters, 112-113,* 153-156.

McGuire, P.K., Cope, H.M., and Fahy, T. (1994). Diverse psychiatric morbidity associated with useof 3,4-methylene-dioxymethamphetamine ('ecstasy'). *British Journal of Psychiatry, 165,* 391-394.

McKetin, R., and Mattick, R.P. (1998). Attention and memory in illicit amphetamine users: comparison with non-drug-using controls. *Drug and Alcohol Dependence, 50,* 181-184.

Meyer, S., Kleinschmidt, S., Gottschling, S., Gortner, L., and Stittmatter, M. (2005). Gamma-hydroxy butyric acid: neurotransmitter, sedative and party drug. *Wien Med Wochenschr,*155, 315-322.

Morgan, C.J., Monaghan, L., and Curran, H.V. (2004a). Beyond the K-hole: A 3-year longitudinal investigation of the cognitive and subjective effects of ketamine in recreational users who have substantially reduced their use of the drug. *Addiction, 99,* 1450-1461.

Morgan, C.J.A., Riccelli, M., Maitland, C.H., and Curran, H.V. (2004b). Long-term effects of ketamine: evidence for a persisting impairment of source memory in recreational users. *Drug and Alcohol Dependence, 75,* 301-308.

National Institute on Drug Abuse. (2001). *NIDA Research Report Series: Prescription Drugs Abuse and Addiction.* Bethesda, MD: National Institutes of Health.

National Institute on Drug Abuse. (2005). *NIDA Info Facts: Club Drugs.* Bethesda, MD: National Institutes of Health.

Nixon, S.J. and Bowlby, D.C. (1996). Evidence of alcohol-related efficiency deficits in an episodic learning task. *Alcoholism: Clinical and Experimental Research, 20,* 21-24.

Nixon, S.J. and Parsons, O.A. (1991). Alcohol-related efficiency deficits using an ecologically valid test. *Alcoholism: Clinical and Experimental Research, 15,* 601-606.

Nixon, S.J., Paul, R., and Phillips, M. (1998). Cognitive efficiency in alcoholics and polysubstance abusers. *Alcoholism: Clinical and Experimental Research, 22,* 1414-1420.

Nixon, S.J., Tivis, R., Ceballos, N., Varner, J.L., and Rohrbaugh, J. (2002). Neurophysiological efficiency in male and female alcoholics. *Progress in Neuro-Psychopharmacology and Biological Psychiatry, 26,* 919-927.

Nordahl, T.E., Salo, R., and Leamon, M. (2003). Neuropsychological effects of chronic methamphetamine use on neurotransmitters and cognition: A review. *The Journal of Neuropsychiatry and Clinical Neurosciences, 15,* 317-325.

O'Malley, S., Adams, M., Heaton, R.K., and Gawin, F.H. (1992). Neuropsychological impairment in chronic cocaine abusers. *American Journal on Alcohol and Drug Abuse, 18,* 131-144.

Parrot, A.C., and Lasky, J. (1998). Ecstasy (MDMA) effects upon mood and cognition: before, during and after a Saturday night dance. *Psychopharmacology, 139,* 261-268.

Parrot, A., Lees, A., Garnham, N., Jones, M., and Wesnes, K. (1998). Cognitive performance in recreational users of MDMA or 'ecstasy': Evidence for memory deficits. *Journal of Psychopharmacology, 12,* 79-83.

Parrott, A.C. (2004). MDMA (3,4-methylenedioxymethamphetamine) or Ecstasy: The neuropsychological implications of taking it at dances and raves. *Neuropsychobiology, 50,* 329-335.

Patrick, G., Straumanis, J.J., Struve, F.A., Fitz-Gerald, M.J., and Manno, J.E. (1997). Early and middle latency evoked potentials in medically and psychiatrically normal daily marijuana users: a paucity of significant findings. *Clinical Electroencephalography, 28,* 26-31.

Paulus, M.P., Hozack, N., Frank, L., Brown, G.G., and Schuckit, M.A. (2003). Decision making by methamphetamine-dependent subjects is associated with error-rate-independent decrease in prefrontal and parietal activation. *Biological Psychiatry, 53,* 65-74.

Pope, H.G., Gruber, A.J., Hudson, J.I., Huestis, M.A., and Yurgelun-Todd, D. (2002). Cognitive measures in long-term cannabis users. *Journal of Clinical Pharmacology, 42,* 41S-47S.

Pope, H.G., Gruber, A.J., and Yugelun-Todd, D. (1995). The residual neuropsychological effects of cannabis: The current status of research. *Drug and Alcohol Dependence, 38,* 25-34.

Potter, J.S., Hennessy, G., Borrow, J.A., Greenfield, S.F., and Weiss, R.D. (2004). Substance use histories in patients seeking treatment for controlled-release oxycodone dependence. *Drug and Alcohol Dependence, 76,* 213-215.

Regier, D.A., Farmer, M.E., Rae, D.A., Locke, B.Z., Keith, S.J., Judd, L.L., and Goodwin, F.K. (1990). Comorbidity of mental disorder with alcohol and other drug abuse. Results from the Epidemiologic Catchment Area (ECA) Study. *Journal of The American Medical Association, 264,* 2511-2518.

Reid, M.C., Engles-Horton, L.L., Weber, M.B., Kerns, R.D., Rogers, E.L., and O'Connor, P.G. (2002). Use of opioid medications for chronic noncancer pain syndromes in primary care. *Journal of General Internal Medicine, 17,* 173-179.

Reneman, L., Booij, J., Schmand, B., van den Brink, W., and Gunning, B. (2000). Memory disturbances in ecstasy users are correlated with an altered brain serotonin neurotransmission. *Psychopharmacology, 148,* 322-324.

Reneman, L., Lavalaye, J., Schmand, B., de Wolff, F.A., van den Brink, W., den Heeten, G.J., and Booij, J. (2001). Cortical serotonin transporter density and verbal memory in individuals who stopped using 3,4-methylenedioxymethamphetamine (MDMA or "Ecstasy"): preliminary findings. *Archives of General Psychiatry, 58,* 901-906.

Ricaurte, G., and McCann, U.D. (2005). Recognition and management of complications of new recreational drug use. *Lancet, 365*, 2137-2145.

Ricaurte, G.A., Yuan, J., and McCann, D.U. (2000). 3,4-methylenedioxy-methaphetamine (ecstasy)-induced serotonin neurotoxicity: studies in animals. *Neuropsychobiology, 42*, 5-10.

Robbins, L.N., Cottler, L., Bucholz, K., and Compton, W. (1995). *The Diagnostic Interview Schedule, Version IV.* St. Louis, MO: Washington University.

Robinson, J.E., Heaton, R.K., and O'Malley, S.S. (1999). Neuropsychological functioning in cocaine abusers with and without alcohol dependence. *Journal of the International Neuropsychological Society, 5*, 10-9.

Rodgers, J. (2001). Cognitive performance amongst recreational users of "ecstasy". *Psychopharmacology, 151*, 19-24.

Rodgers, J., Buchanan, T., Scholey, A.B., Heffernan, T.M., Ling, J., and Parrott, A.C. (2003). Patterns of drug use and the influence of gender on self-reports of memory ability in ecstasy users: a web-based study. *Journal of Psychopharmacology, 17*, 389-396.

Rogers, R.D., and Robbins RW. (2001). Investigating the neurocognitive deficits associated with chronic drug misuse. *Current Opinion in Neurobiology, 11*, 250-257.

Salo R., Nordahl T.E., Possin K., Leamon M., Gibson D.R., Galloway G.P., Flynn N.M., Henik A., Pfefferbaum A., and Sullivan E. (2002). Preliminary evidence of reduced cognitive inhibition in methamphetamine-dependent individuals. *Psychiatry Research, 111*, 65-74.

Simon, S.L., Domier, C., Carnell, J., Brethen, P., Rawson, R., and Ling, W. (2000). Cognitive impairment in individuals currently using methamphetamine. *The American Journal on Addictions, 9*, 216-221.

Simon, S.L., Domier, C.P., Sim, T., Richardson, K., Rawson, R.A., and Ling, W. (2002a). Cognitive performance of current methamphetamine and cocaine abusers. *Journal of Addictive Disorders, 21*, 61-74.

Simon, S.L., Richardson, K., Dacey, J., Glynn, S., Domier, C.P., Rawson, R.A., and Ling, W. (2002b). A comparison of patterns of methamphetamine and cocaine use. *Journal of Addictive Diseases, 21*, 35-44.

Simoni-Wastila, L. (2000). The use of abusable prescription drugs: The role of gender. *Journal of Womens Health and Gender Based Medicine, 9*, 289-297.

Spielberger, C.D. (1983). *Manual for the State-Trait Anxiety Inventory.* Palo Alto, CA: Consulting Psychologists Press.

Stahl, M. (2000). *Essential pharmacology: Neuroscientific basis and practical application, 2nd Edition.* Cambridge: Cambridge University Press.

Stevens, M.C., Kaplan, R.F., and Bauer, L.O. (2001). Relationship of cognitive ability to the developmental course of antisocial behavior in substance-dependent patients. *Progress in Neuro-Psychopharmacology and Biological Psychiatry, 25,* 1523-36.

Strickland, T.L., and Stein, R. (1995). Cocaine-induced cerebrovascular impairment: challenges to neuropsychological assessment. *Neuropsychology Review, 5,* 69-79.

Substance Abuse and Mental Health Services Administration (SAMHSA). (2000). *Trends in Substance Abuse Treatment Admissions: 1992-2000.* Available at: *http://www.samhsa.gov/teds00/TEDS_2k_Chp2.htm.*

Substance Abuse and Mental Health Services Administration. Office of Applied Studies. (2005). *Results from the 2004 National Survey on Drug Use and Health: National Findings.* Available at: http://www .oas.samhsa.gov/NSDUH/2k4NSDUH/ 2k4results/2k4results.htm.

Sullivan, E.V., Desmond, J.E., Lim, K.O., and Pfefferbaum, A. (2002). Speed and efficiency, but not accuracy or timing deficits of limb movement in alcoholic men and women. *Alcoholism: Clinical and Experimental Research, 26,* 705-713.

Tedstone, D. and Coyle, K. (2004). Cognitive impairments in sober alcoholics: performance on selective and divided attention tasks. *Drug and Alcohol Dependence, 75,* 277-286.

United States Department of Health and Human Services. (2004). *Oxycodone, hydrocodone, and polydrug use, 2002 Drug Abuse Warning Network Publication.* Rockville, MD: United States Department of Health and Human Services.

Verdejo-Garcia, A.J., Lopez-Torrecillas, F., Agular de Arcos, F., and Perez-Garcia, M. (2005). Differential effects of MDMA, cocaine, and cannabis use severity on distinctive components of the executive functions in polysubstance users: multiple regression analysis. *Addictive Behaviors, 30,* 89-101.

Verdejo, A., Toribio, I., and Orozco, C. (2005). Neuropsychological functioning in methadone maintenance patients versus abstinent heroin abusers. *Drug and Alcohol Dependence, 78,* 283-288.

Verkes, R.J., Gijsman, H.J., Pieters, R.C., de Visser, S., Kuijpers, M., Pennings, J.M., de Bruin, D., Van de Weinjngaart, G., Van Grven, J.M.A., and Cohen, A.F. (2001). Cognitive performance and serotonergic function in users of ecstasy. *Psychopharmacology, 153,* 196-202.

Vik, P.W., Cellucci, T., Jarchow, M.S., and Hedt, J. (2004). Cognitive impairment in substance abuse. *Psychiatric Clinics of North America, 27,* 97-109.

Wang, G.J., Volkow, N.D., Chang, L., Miller, E., Sedler, M., Hitzemann, R., Zhu, W., Logan, J., Ma,Y., and Fowler, J.S. (2004). Partial recovery of brain metabolism in methamphetamine abusers after protracted abstinence. *American Journal of Psychiatry, 161,* 242-248.

Wareing, M., Fisk, J.E., and Murphy, P.N. (2000). Working memory deficits in current and previous users of MDMA ("ecstasy"). *British Journal of Psychology, 91,* 181-188.

Wareing, M., Murphy, P.N., and Fisk, J.E. (2004). Visuospatial memory impairments in users of MDMA ("ecstasy"). *Psychopharmacology, 173,* 391-397.

Warner, E.A. (1993). Cocaine abuse. *Annals of Internal Medicine, 199,* 226-236.

Wolf, B. C., Lavezzi, W. A., Sullivan, L. M., and Flannagan, L. M. (2005). *Journal of Forensic Sciences, 50,* 192-195.

Zachary, P.A. (1986). *Shipley Institute of Living Scale – Revised Manual.* Los Angeles, CA: Western Psychological Services.

Zacny, J.P., and Gutierrez, S. (2003). Characterizing the subjective, psychomotor and physiological effects of oral oxycodone in non-drug-abusing volunteers. *Psychopharmacology, 170,* 242-254.

Zakzanis, K.K., and Young, D.A. (2001). Memory impairment in abstinent MDMA ("ecstasy") users: a longitudinal investigation. *Neurology, 56,* 966-969.

In: Substance Abuse among Adolescents   ISBN: 978-1-61122-933-2
Editor: Isabelle M. Giordano   © 2011 Nova Science Publishers, Inc.

Chapter 7

MEMORY AND EXECUTIVE DEFICITS IN EARLY ABSTINENCE FROM ALCOHOL

J. Uekermann, K. Luken, V. Taneva, W. Vollmoeller[1] and I. Daum*

Institute of Cognitive Neuroscience, Ruhr-University of Bochum, Germany
[1] Westfälisches Zentrum für Psychiatrie und Psychotherapie, Germany

ABSTRACT

Background: Studies on neuropsychological functioning in alcoholism have reported cognitive changes, which have been interpreted in light of the frontal lobe hypothesis and the hypothesis of global brain dysfunction. Findings concerning the influence of family history of alcoholism on cognitive functions are inconsistent. Since cognitive functions may be relevant for the therapy of alcoholism, investigations of alcoholics in early abstinence are of critical importance.

Methods: Alcoholic patients (A) in early abstinence and healthy controls (C) were compared on a range of cognitive domains, including verbal and visual memory, prospective memory, memory for temporal

---

* Correspondence to be addressed to Jennifer Uekermann, Faculty of Psychology, Institute of Cognitive Neuroscience; GAFO 05/607, Ruhr-University of Bochum, 44780 Bochum, Germany; Email: *Jennifer.Uekermann@ruhr-uni-bochum.de*; Telephone:+49-234-32-23119; Telefax: +49-234-32-14622

order and executive functions (working memory, planning, verbal fluency). Analyses included a comparison of A and C. In addition, the cognitive profile of alcoholics with a positive (F+) and negative family history of alcoholism (F-) was compared.

Results: Group comparisons yielded verbal and visual memory deficits of alcoholics. Alcoholics were also impaired on alternate and phonemic verbal fluency. The two alcoholic subgroups with and without a positive family history did not differ significantly from each other on any cognitive measure.

Conclusions: The observed impairments in early abstinence are consistent with the hypothesis of diffuse brain dysfunction. Future studies using multidimensional designs are desirable to investigate the influence of family history on neuropsychological functions and the association between cognitive measures and relapse in further detail.

INTRODUCTION

Alcoholism is associated with a range of cognitive deficits (Parsons, 1994), which are thought to be related to functional and structural changes in the prefrontal cortex (see Moselhy et al. 2001). Current literature focuses on the "frontal lobe-hypothesis" of alcoholism, which suggests that the prefrontal cortex is particularly vulnerable to the effects of alcohol. According to the hypothesis of diffuse brain dysfunction alcoholism is associated with a global dysfunction of the brain and consequently leads to a more variable impairment patterns (see Parsons, 1994).

Evidence from neuropsychological studies supports the frontal lobe hypothesis (e.g. Uekermann et al., 2003). In these investigations, executive deficits relating to verbal fluency, inhibition, abstraction and reasoning have been frequently observed (Dao-Castellana et al, 1998; Beatty et al., 2000). Ihara et al. (2000) administered the "behavioral assessment of the dysexecutive syndrome" (Wilson et al., 1996), and reported pronounced executive impairment in two thirds of the patients on this ecologically valid test battery.

The identification and rehabilitation of cognitive deficits may have implications for the therapy of alcoholism. Executive functions are predictors for abstinence (Curran et al., 2000; Teichner, et al., 2001) and memory impairments have also been associated with poorer treatment compliance (Guthrie and Elliott, 1980). Blume et al. (2005) reported that higher memory scores predicted readiness to change drinking behaviour. Specific memory impairments are observed after damage to the prefrontal cortex (see Mayes,

1988), with poor free recall, poor memory for temporal order and prospective memory as well as high false alarms rates (see Daum and Mayes, 2000).

There is evidence that cognitive functions show recovery after cessation of drinking. Although recovery is incomplete (see Moselhy et al., 2001) significant abstinence effects have been observed for abstraction and perceptual motor speed (Mann et al., 1999). Abstinence effects have also been found in imaging studies. Johnson-Greene et al. (1997) reported partial recovery of glucose metabolism in the prefrontal cortex which was related to improvements of executive function.

Most studies assessed cognitive deficits several weeks or months after detoxification. Since treatment success may be affected by cognitive status, studies in early abstinence are of critical importance. In a recent study by Zinn et al. (2004) of alcoholic patients in early abstinence, patients showed reasoning and memory deficits as well as reduced psychomotor speed. Patients and healthy controls, however, also differed on general intellectual functioning, which was (partly) related to executive deficits. Prospective memory and memory for temporal order, which are closely related to the prefrontal cortex, were not assessed.

Another issue concerns the relationship between parental substance abuse, subsequent alcohol problems and cognitive deficits. In several studies, the cognitive performance of alcoholic patients with a positive family history (F+) was compared to alcoholic patients with a negative family history of alcoholism (F-). The results are inconsistent. In an early investigation by Schaeffer et al. (1984), F+ patients showed poorer abstraction/problem solving performance than F- patients. Schafer et al. (1991) did not observe significant relationships between family history of alcoholism and cognitive functions. F+ and F- patients also did not differ on neuropsychological and neuroimaging variables in a later study (Adams et al., 1998). By contrast Keenan et al. (1997) observed more neurological soft signs (blunt vs. sharp discrimination, dysdiadochokinesis and graphestesia) in F+ patients when compared to F- patients.

These inconsistencies may be relatated to differences in study designs and definition of family history of alcoholism. In some of the previous investigations, alcoholics with a positive family history of maternal drinking were also included. Maternal history of alcoholism may be associated with fetal alcohol syndrome, including central nervous system dysfunction, abnormal facial features, behavioural deficits and growth deficiency (Jones and Smith, 1973). In addition, some investigation were based on correlational analyses and/or F+ and F- alcoholics were not comparable on age, general intellectual functioning, disease duration, and duration of abstinence.

The aim of the present study was to assess memory and executive deficits in early abstinence and the influence of paternal family history on cognitive functions in alcoholism. Alcoholic patients with positive and negative paternal history of alcoholism in early abstinence were compared on a range of executive (verbal fluency, planning, working memory) and memory functions (verbal, visual, prospective memory, memory for temporal order).

METHOD

Participants

Two groups participated in the present investigation. The first group (A) consisted of 31 alcoholic patients (28 men, 3 women). Alcoholism was diagnosed according to DSM-IV (Sass et al., 1996). At the time of testing alcoholics were inpatients in the "Westfälisches Zentrum für Psychiatrie und Psychotherapie" of the Ruhr-University Bochum. Exclusion criteria were a history of neurological illness, psychotic symptoms, head trauma, dementia, anoxia, seizures or delirium tremens in the last weeks and age > 60. Patients were 43,65 (SD = 7,34) years on average. Present state intellectual function, as assessed by the Similarities and Picture Completion subtests of the Reduced Wechsler Intelligence Scales (WIP; Dahl, 1972) was 115,94 (SD = 9,35). A scored 11,19 (SD = 8,45) on average on the Beck Depression Inventory (Beck, 1987). Mean duration of alcoholism was 8,81 (SD = 6,85 years; range 1-25 years). Patients were abstinent from alcohol for 10,61 (SD = 2,61; range 9-24) days on average. Medication of the patient group consisted of vitamine B (n = 15), antiepileptic medication (Magnerot, Tegretal, Valproat, Tiapridex; n = 20), antidepressant medication (Trimineurin, Cipramil, Remergil, Cypralex; n = 15), medication for the treatment of blood pressure (n = 9) and insuline (n = 1). Patients underwent a short interview, in which history of alcoholism (duration, family history) was assessed. Patients who reported a positive maternal history were excluded because of possible fetal alcohol effects. For further analyses alcoholic patients were divided in a group with positive (F+; n = 15; 14 men, 1 female) and negative paternal drinking history (F-, n = 16; 14 male, 2 female). The patient groups did not differ significantly on age, IQ estimate, depression score, disease duration or abstinence (all p >.11).

The control group (C) consisted of 18 healthy participants (14 men, 4 female). Exclusion criteria were neurological and psychiatric diseases, anoxia, dementia. head trauma and age > 60. Mean age was 40,06 (SD = 10,62) years. The C group had a mean score of 118,22 (SD =) on the WIP and 4,78 (SD = 4,02) on the BDI.

The two groups did not differ significantly on age or IQ estimate (both p > .17). The A group scored significantly higher on the BDI (Chi = 6,87; p = .009). When C was compared to the two alcoholic subgroups (F+ and F-), no significant group differences concerning age and IQ emerged (both p > .16). BDI scores of F- and F+ were significantly higher in comparison to C (both p < .05).

Informed consent was obtained from all participants after the purpose and procedure of the study had been fully explained to them. The study was approved by the ethics committee of the Ruhr-University, Bochum, Germany and performed in accordance with the guidelines of the Declaration of Helsinki.

Neuropsychological Assessment

Neuropsychological assessment included attention, verbal memory, visual memory, prospective memory, memory for temporal order and executive functions.

Attention was measured by the forward Digit Span task of the Wechsler Intelligence Scales (Wechsler, 1981). Digit sequences are read aloud by the experimenter and the participant has to reproduce them immediately thereafter. The dependent variable is the number of correctly reproduced digits.

MEMORY ASSESSMENT

Verbal Memory

Verbal memory was assessed by the prose passage of the Wechsler Memory Scale-R (WMS-R; Wechsler, 1987, Härting, 2000). A story is read aloud by the experimenter and has to be reproduced immediately thereafter and again after a 30-minute delay. Analyses included the number of correctly reproduced items during immediate and delayed recall.

Visual Memory

Visual Memory was assessed by the Rey Osterrieth figure (Osterrieth, 1944), the dot-lines task (Daum and Mayes, 2000) and the pattern-recall subtest of the Berlin Amnesia Test (Metzler et al., 1992).

The first task involves the presentation of a complex figure, which has to be copied. After a 40 minutes delay, the figure has to be reproduced from memory. Dependent variable is the number of correctly reproduced details of the figure.

The dot-lines task (Daum and Mayes, 2000) includes four geometrical figures, which consist of four dots which are connected by straight lines. The figures have to be copied and reproduced after 30 minutes. In the second condition, five further patterns have to be copied and recognized after 30 minutes among 15 distracters. Analyses included the number of correctly reproduced and recognized items

Memory for Temporal Order

Memory for temporal order was assessed using faces from the Recognition Memory Test (RMTF) (Warrington, 1984) and the procedure described by Daum and Mayes (2000). Two sets of photographs (A and B), which consisted of 12 faces each are shown with a delay of 2 minutes between sets. After a 30 minutes delay, faces had to be recognized among 24 distractors. In addition, participants have to indicate, whether the face was shown in set A or B during encoding. Dependent variables are the recognition index ((hits-false alarms)/number of stimuli) and the temporal order index (number of correctly ordered items/number of hits).

Prospective Memory

Prospective memory was assessed by three subtests. In the "object-task" the experimenter hides an object at the beginning of the neuropsychological assessment. The participant is instructed to ask the experimenter for the object during the first interval. In the second task, the participant is instructed to ask the experimenter whether he is allowed to use his mobile phone during the first interval. In addition, the participant is instructed to go into the patients' group room after neuropsychological assessment, to come back to the experimenter's room and to tell the experimenter about the current TV program. The dependent variable is the number of correctly completed tasks.

MEASURES OF EXECUTIVE FUNCTION

Planning

Planning was measured by the Modified Six Elements Subtest of the BADS (Wilson, 1996). The MSET includes three subtests (dictation, arithmetic and picture naming). Each test consists of two parts, A and B. Participants are told that they are not allowed to do parts A and B of a test one after the other. In addition, they have to carry out at least part of each test within ten minutes. Analyses include the number of rule breaks as well as a total score reflecting overall performance.

Working Memory

Working memory was assessed by the backward digit spans of the Wechsler Intelligence Scales (Wechsler, 1981). Participants are instructed to reproduce series of numbers backwards. Dependent variable is the number of correctly reproduced numbers.

Verbal Fluency

Verbal fluency was assessed by three tasks (Daum et al., 1995). In the semantic task, participants are asked to produce as many country names as possible within a time limit of one minute. In the phonemic condition, as many nouns as possible beginning with the letter "b" have to be produced within one minute. In the alternate subtest, subjects are instructed to alternately produce male first names and vegetables within one minute. Dependent variables include the number of correct exemplars in each condition.

Data Analyses

In a first analysis step, neuropsychological performance of alcoholic patients (A) was compared to the healthy control group (C) by t-tests for independent groups for normally distributed raw test scores. Data analyses where the normal distribution criterion was not met were performed using nonparametric Mann-Whitney-U- Test. In the second analysis step, the two alcoholic subgroups (F+ and F-) were compared by t-tests or Mann-Whitney-U-Test, respectively. Verbal memory performance was analysed by repeated measure analysis with group (A and C) and delay (immediate versus delayed recall) as factors. For the investigation of the relation between clinical, affective and cognitive measures, Pearson correlation coefficients were completed.

RESULTS

Comparison between A and C

Attention

The results for digit span forward are shown in table 1.

Table 1. Results (means and SDs) for attention and memory in the two groups

	A	C
Attention		
Digit Span Forward (baseline)	7,23 (2,11)	8,00 (2,27)
Visual Memory		
Dot-line task (recall)	1,52 (1,12)	2,17 (0,86)
Dot-line task (recognition)	3,90 (1,27)	4,33 (1,08)
RMTF recognition index	0,64 (0,19)	0,78 (0,16)
RMTF temporal order index	0,59 (0,14)	0,62 (0,17)
Prospective memory	2,13 (0,85)	2,56 (0,51)
Executive functions		
Modified Six Elements Test	3,26 (0,93)	3,50 (0,62)
Digit Span backward	6,74 (2,28)	7,78 (2,73)
Semantic verbal fluency	23,00 (10,24)	27,67 (10,08)

No significant differences emerged ($p = .33$).

Verbal Memory

The data for verbal memory are shown in figure 1.

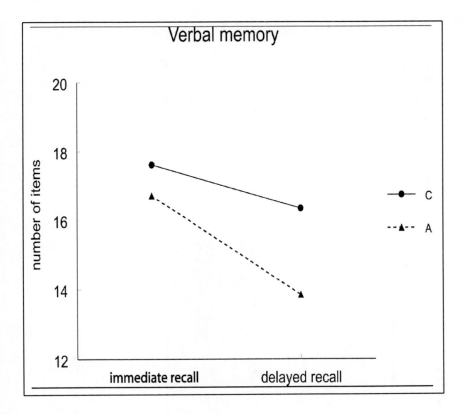

Figure 1. Results for the verbal memory task.

Repeated measure analyses with group (A versus C) and delay (immediate versus delayed) yielded a significant effect of delay (F $(1,47)$ = 29,80; p < .0001) as well as a significant group X delay interaction (F $(1, 47)$ = 4,39; p = .04). Subsequent Tukey test of forgetting rate ((delayed recall/-immediate recall)/ immediate recall) showed that the forgetting rates of A were significantly higher (p = .03).

Visual Memory

The data for delayed recall of the Rey Osterrieth figure is shown in figure 2.

Group A recalled significantly fewer items in comparison with C (t (47) = - 3,58; p =.001).

The results for the dot line task are shown in table 1. A significant group difference emerged for the recall condition (Chi = 4,56; p = .03), which was due to significantly lower scores of A in comparison with C. Analysis of the recognition condition did not yield significant differences (p = .23).

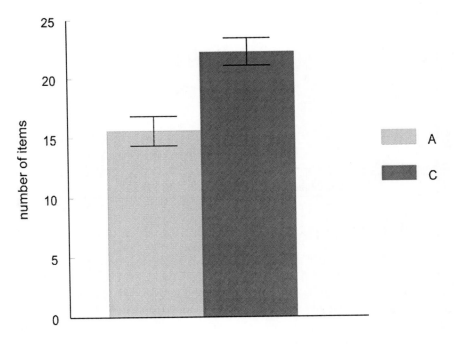

Figure 2. Results (means and standard errors) for delayed recall of the Rey Osterrieth Figure.

Memory for Temporal Order

The results for the recogniton and the temporal order index are shown in table 1. Analyses yielded significant differences for the recognition index (t (47) = -2,39; p = .02), which was due to poorer memory of group A when compared to C. Analyses of the temporal order index did not yield significant differences (p = .51).

Prospective Memory

The data for prospective memory are shown in table 1. No significant differences emerged.

Executive Function

The results for working memory, the modified Six Elements Test and the semantic verbal
memory tasks are shown in table 1.
Analyses did not yield any significant group difference (all p > .28).
Data for the phonemic and alternate verbal fluency tasks are illustrated in figure 3.

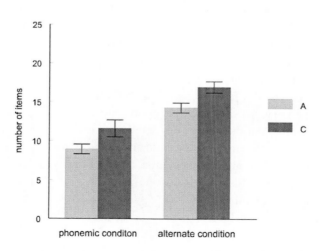

Figure 3. Results (means and standard errors) for phonemic and alternate verbal fluency.

Analyses yielded significant effects (Chi = 6,35; p = .01; t (47) = -2,66; p = .01). A scored significantly lower on phonemic and alternate verbal fluency.

Comparison between Alcoholic Subgroups

Comparison between both alcoholic subgroups did not yield any significant results.

Influence of Medication

Comparisons of medicated and unmedicated patients did not reveal any significant difference.

Correlational Analyses

Correlational analyses did not yield any significant correlations between the BDI, duration of abstinence, disease duration and cognitive measures (all p > .16).

DISCUSSION

The results of the present investigation indicate visual and verbal memory as well as mild executive deficits in alcoholics early in the course of abstinence. Visual memory deficits were reflected in a reduced number of recognised faces of the Recognition Memory Test and a reduced number of reproduced items of the Rey Osterrieth figure. In addition, alcoholics scored significantly lower on the recall condition of the dot line task. Verbal memory impairments were reflected by a significantly higher forgetting rate of the story during delayed recall. The recognition condition of the dot line task, prospective memory, memory for temporal order and attention were not affected. Executive deficits were restricted to the alternate and phonemic condition of verbal fluency. No significant impairments were observed for working memory, planning and semantic verbal fluency. Alcoholics with a positive and negative history of alcoholism (F+ and F-) did not differ significantly from each other.

Although clear conclusions about brain localisation on the basis of behavioural data are limited, the deficits may be interpreted in the light of the frontal lobe hypothesis, which suggests a particular vulnerability of the prefrontal cortex to the toxic effects of alcohol. This interpretation is in line with data from imaging studies, which have shown activation of the prefrontal cortex during active encoding and retrieval (Shallice et al., 1994). Leube et al. (2003) reported left medial frontal/anterior cingulate cortex activation in a face recognition task. Herrmann et al. (2003) observed activation of the right and left prefrontal cortex during verbal fluency. In addition, Dao-Castellana et al. (1998) reported verbal fluency deficits in alcoholics, which were related to mediofrontal hypometabolism.

Executive deficits could be of particular relevance for the treatment of alcoholism. In this context, the heuristic model of alcohol addiction by Giancola and Moss (1998) is of importance. The model is based on the supervisory attentional and contention scheduling system distinction by Shallice (1988). The contention scheduling system is responsible for the execution of stereotypic and overlearned behaviour (behaviour which is related to alcoholism such as seeking for alcohol, drinking alcohol) whereas the supervisory attentional system is activated when stereotypic behaviour (e.g. novel adaptive strategies to establish abstinence) is inadequate. In the light of the memory and executive deficits of patients with alcoholism specific treatment programmes, which account for these deficits may be useful.

In the present investigation executive deficits were restricted to alternate and phonemic verbal fluency, whereas working memory, semantic verbal fluency, planning and prospective memory were preserved. Alcoholics also suffered from a range of memory deficits, which was reflected by a reduced number of recognised faces of the Recognition Memory Test, a reduced number of reproduced items of the Rey Osterrieth figure and dot line task, as well as a higher verbal memory forgetting rate. These findings are consistent with other investigations, which have reported a detrimental effect of alcohol on memory formation (e.g. Ryback, 1970; 1971). The observed memory deficits can be further interpreted in the context of investigations, which suggest hippocampal pathology in alcoholism (Errico et al., 2002; Nixon and Crews, 2004). Memory deficits could influence the ability to benefit from information in rehabilitation and to remember future tasks and may thus contribute to outcome of therapy of alcoholism. This assumption is supported by studies, in which associations between memory impairments and poorer treatment compliance was reported (Blume et al., 2005; Guthrie and Elliott, 1980). In summary, the observed impairment pattern in early abstinence is consistent with the hypothesis of global brain dysfunction (see Parsons, 1994).

The observed deficits of alcoholics cannot be due to differences concerning age, intellectual functioning or affective variables since both groups were comparable in this regard.

One limitation of the study is the fact that history of alcoholism involved duration of disease and abstinence only and did not include a more detailed assessment of drinking variables such as maximum and average alcohol consumption per day and age at first intoxification. In addition, sample sizes were relatively small, which is due to strict matching and selection criteria. One further limitation concerns the fact that only three women were included in the study. The investigation of executive functions and memory in female patients with alcoholism would be of particular relevance in the light of studies which have suggested a greater vulnerability to alcohol neurotoxicity among females (Hommer et al., 2001).

The alcoholic subgroups (F+ and F-) did not differ significantly on any measure. This finding is inconsistent with previous studies, in which more severe cognitive deficits and neurological soft signs were observed in alcoholics with a positive history of alcoholism (Keenan et al.; 1997; Schaeffer et al., 1984). However, in these investigations patients with maternal history of alcoholism were also included. In addition, alcoholic subgroups also differed significantly concerning duration of disease in the study by Schaeffer et al. (1984). In the present study alcoholic subgroups were comparable with respect to age, intellectual functioning, duration of abstinence and disease. The lack of significant differences between alcoholics with a positive and negative family history of alcoholism is consistent with other investigations, who did not report a significant influence. Beatty et al. (2000) reported impairments of alcoholics on the Shipley Vocabulary and abstraction test. Patients with positive and negative family history, however, did not differ significantly from each other. Adams et al. (1998) administered neuropsychological tests and neuroimaging and did not find an influence of familiy history of alcoholism.

The results of the present investigation are consistent with Adams et al. (1998) who concluded that "family history of alcoholism does not moderate the damaging effects of severe chronic alcoholism." An alternative explanation could be the assumption that a range of medical, psychiatric and disease variables contribute to the cognitive performance of alcoholics. Thus a multidimensional approach would be necessary to allow clear conclusions concerning the influence of family history of alcoholism.

In summary, the results of the present investigation suggest memory and executive deficits in alcoholics in early abstinence, which may influence therapy of alcoholism. Future studies using multidimensional and longitudinal designs are desirable to investigate the influence of family history on neuropsychological functions and the association between cognitive measures and relapse in further detail.

REFERENCES

Adams, K.M., Gilman, S., Johnson-Greene, D., Koeppe, R.A., Junck, L., Kluin, K.J., Martorello, S., Johnson, M.J., Heumann, M., and Hill, E. (1998). The significance of family history status in relation to neuropsychological test performance and cerebral glucose metabolism studied with positron emission tomography in older alcoholic patients. *Alcoholism: Clinical and Experimental Research, 22*, 105-10.

Beatty, W.W., Tivis, R., Stott, H.D., Nixon, S.J., and Parsons, O.A. (2000). Neuropsychological deficits in sober alcoholics: influences of chronicity and recent alcohol consumption. *Alcoholism: Clinical and Experimental Research, 24*, 149-54.

Beck, A.T. (1987). *Beck Depression Inventory*. San Antonio, TX: The Psychological Corporation.

Blume, A.W., Schmaling, K.B., and Marlatt, G.A. (2005). Memory, executive cognitive function, and readiness to change drinking behavior. *Addictive Behaviours, 30*, 301-3014.

Curran, G.M., Flynn, H.A., Kirchner, J., and Booth, B.M. (2000). Depression after alcohol treatment as a risk factor for relapse among male veterans. *Journal of Substance Abuse Treatment, 19,* 259-65.

Dahl, G. (1972). *Reduzierter Wechlser Intelligenztest* (Short version of the Wechsler intelligence test). Meisenheim: Verlag Anton Hain.

Dao – Castellana, M.H., Samson, Y., Legault, F., Martinot, J.L., Aubin, H.J., Crouzel, C., Feldman, L., Barrucandm, D., Rancurel, G., Féline, A., and Syrota, A. (1998). Frontal dysfunction in neurologically normal chronic alcoholic subjects: metabolic and neuropsychological findings. *Psychological Medicine, 28*, 1049-1062.

Daum, I., Schugens, M.M., Spieker, S., Poser, U., Schonle, P.W., and Birbaumer, N. (1995). Memory and skill acquisition in Parkinson's disease and frontal lobe dysfunction. *Cortex, 31*, 413-432.

Daum, I., and Mayes, A.R. (2000). Memory and executive function impairments after frontal or posterior cortex lesions. *Behavioral Neurology, 12*, 161-173.

Errico, A.L., King, A.C., Lovallo, W.R., and Parsons, O.A. (2002). Cortisol dysregulation and cognitive impairment in abstinent male alcoholics. *Alcoholism: Clinical and Experimental Research, 26*, 1198-204.

Giancola, P.R., and Moss, H.B. (1998). Executive cognitive functioning in alcohol use disorders. *Recent Developments in Alcoholism, 14*, 227-51.

Guthrie, A., and Elliott, W.A. (1980). The nature and reversibility of cerebral impairment in alcoholism; treatment implications. *Journal of Studies on Alcohol, 41*, 147-55.

Härting, C., Markowitsch, H.J., Neufeld, H., Calabrese, P., and Deisinger, K. (2000). *WMS-R. Wechsler Gedächtnis Test. Deutsche Adaptation der revidierten Fassung der Wechsler-Memory-Scale.* Göttingen: Hogrefe.

Herrmann, M.J., Ehlis, A.C., and Fallgatter, A.J. (2003). Frontal activation during a verbal-fluency task as measured by near-infrared spectroscopy. *Brain Research Bulletin, 61*, 51-6.

Hommer, D., Momenan, R., Kaiser, E., and Rawlings, R. (2001). Evidence for a gender-related effect of alcoholism on brain volumes. *American Journal of Psychiatry, 158*, 198-204.

Ihara, H., Berrios, G.E., and London, M. (2000). Group and case study of the dysexecutive syndrome in alcoholism without amnesia. *Journal of Neurology, Neurosurgery and Psychiatry, 68*, 731-7.

Johnson-Greene, D., Adams, K.M., Gilman, S., Koeppe, R.A., Junck, L., Kluin, K.J., Martorello, S., and Heumann, M. (1997). Effects of abstinence and relapse upon neuropsychological function and cerebral glucose metabolism in severe chronic alcoholism. *Journal of Clinical and Experimental Neuropsychology, 19*, 378-85.

Jones, K.L., and Smith, D.W. (1973). Recognition of the fetal alcohol syndrome in early infancy. *Lancet, 2*, 999-1001.

Keenan, E., O'Donnell, C., Sinanan, K., and O'Callaghan, E. (1997). Severity of alcohol dependence and its relationship to neurological soft signs, neuropsychological impairment and family history. *Acta Psychiatrica Scandinavica, 95*, 272-6.

Leube, D.T., Erb, M., Grodd, W., Bartels, M., and Kircher, T.T. (2003). Successful episodic memory retrieval of newly learned faces activates a left fronto-parietal network. *Brain Research: Cognitive Brain Research, 18*, 97-101.

Mann, K., Gunther, A., Stetter, F., and Ackermann, K. (1999). Rapid recovery from cognitive deficits in abstinent alcoholics: a controlled test-retest study. *Alcohol and Alcoholism, 34*, 567-74.

Mayes, A.R. (1988). *Human Organic Memory Disorders.* Cambridge: Cambridge University Press.

Metzler, P., Voshage, J., and Rösler, P. (1992). Berliner Amnesie Test. Göttingen: Hogrefe.

Moselhy, H.F., Georgiou, G., and Kahn, A. (2001). Frontal lobe changes in alcoholism: a review of the literature. *Alcohol and Alcoholism, 36*, 357-68.

Nixon, K., and Crews, F.T. (2004). Temporally specific burst in cell proliferation increases hippocampal neurogenesis in protacted abstinence from alcohol. *Journal of Neuroscience, 24,* 9714-9722.

Osterrieth, P.A. (1944). Le test de copie d'une figure complexe. *Archives de Psychologie, 30,* 206-356.

Parsons, O.A. (1994). Neuropsychological measures and event-related potentials in alcoholics: interrelationships, long-term reliabilities, and prediction of resumption of drinking. *Journal of Clinical Psychology, 50,* 37-46.

Ryback, R.S. (1970). Alcohol amnesia: observations in seven drinking inpatient alcoholics. *Quarterly Journal of Studies on Alcohol, 31,* 616-632.

Ryback, R.S. (1971). The continuum and specifity of the effects of alcohol on memory. *Qarterly Journal of Studies on Alcohol, 32,* 995-1016.

Saß, H., Wittchen, H.U., and Zaudig, M. (1996). *Diagnostisches und statistisches Manual psychischer Störungen (DSM-IV)* (Diagnostical and Statistical Manual of Mental Disorders). Göttingen: Hogrefe.

Schaeffer, K.W., Parsons, O.A., and Yohman, J.R. (1984). Neuropsychological differences between male familial and nonfamilial alcoholics and nonalcoholics. *Alcoholism: Clinical and Experimental Research, 8,* 347-51.

Schafer, K., Butters, N., Smith, T., Irwin, M., Brown, S., Hanger, P., Grant, I., and Schuckit, M. (1991). Cognitive Performance of Alcoholics: A Longitudinal Evaluation of the Role of Drinking History, Depression, Liver Function, Nutrition, and Family History. *Alcoholism: Clinical and Experimental Research, 15,* 653-660.

Shallice, T. (1988). *From neuropsychology to mental structure.* Combridge: Cambridge University Press.

Shallice, T., Fletcher, P., Frith, C.D., Grasby, P., Frackowiak, R.S., and Dolan, R.J. (1994). Brain regions associated with acquisition and retrieval of verbal episodic memory. *Nature, 368,* 633-5.

Teichner, G., Horner, M.D., and Harvey, R.T. (2001). Neuropsychological predictors of the attainment of treatment objectives in substance abuse patients. *International Journal of Neuroscience, 106,* 253-63.

Uekermann J., Daum I., Schlebusch P., Wiebel B., and Trenckmann U. (2003). Depression and cognitive functioning in alcoholism. *Addiction, 98,* 1521-9.

Warrington, E.K. (1984). *Recognition Memory Test.* Windsor, UK.: NFER-Nelson

Wechsler, D. (1987*). WMS-R: Wechsler Memory Scale – Revised (Manual).* San Antonio: The Psychological Corporation.

Wechsler, D. (1981). *WAIS- R Manual.* New York: The Psychological Corporation.

Wilson, B.A., Alderman, N., Burgess, P.W., Emslie, H. and Evans, J.J. (1996). *Behavioural assessment of the dysexecutive syndrome.* Bury St Edmunds: Thames Valley Test Company.

Zinn, S., Stein, R., and Swartzwelder, H.S. (2004). Executive functioning early in abstinence from alcohol. *Alcoholism: Clinical and Experimental Research, 28,* 1338-46.

In: Substance Abuse among Adolescents   ISBN: 978-1-61122-933-2
Editor: Isabelle M. Giordano   © 2011 Nova Science Publishers, Inc.

Chapter 8

WHAT TO DO WITH THE RELENTLESS HUMAN APPETITE FOR PSYCHOTROPIC SUBSTANCES?

Julio Sotelo *

National Institutes of Health of Mexico, Cuernavaca, Mexico

COMMENTARY

The pursuit for happiness is, perhaps, the most common instinct and the most persistent driving force in humans. In fact, the great majority of our goals are directed to this end. However, in spite of all the progress that modern society has developed for entertainment, communications, ease of domestic tasks and improvement of countless ailments, our search for happiness is frequently unfulfilled. Two main evidences point out a huge gap between our everyday activities and our perception of human satisfaction; these are the large proportion of depression among the general population and the identically large proportion of addictions to both, legal and illegal substances. Although the issue of addiction to drugs is extremely complex, it is important to consider the very basic circumstance that the craving for any neurotropic

---

* Julio Sotelo, MD, Director, National Institutes of Health, Periferico Sur 4118, 01900 Mexico City, MEXICO. Phone: (5255) 5652-8285. Fax: (5255) 5135-2229. e-mail: jsotelo@servidor.unam.mx

recreational substance lies in cerebral substrates and responds to the most understandable of human wants; the feeling of pleasure. From cigarette smoking, to alcohol, to psychotropic medicines and illegal drugs there is a continuum; humans become devoted users just because their molecular effects on some areas of the brain. From a simplistic clinical perspective, it is easy to understand the reasons for failure of therapeutic actions in the fight against addictions; any addiction is easy to acquire and awfully difficult to eliminate; most humans are predisposed to them and they are usually a result of the personal search in response to either one of two ubiquitous feelings; sadness or desire for happiness.

Research on the neural mechanisms involved in addiction should be increased, particularly directed to prevention in those subjects prone to addiction due to genetic or constitutional susceptibility. Comprehensive multidisciplinary approaches must be implemented because most singular interventions currently used, either medical, social or judicial have been largely ineffective.

The brain encompasses all biological substrata for sensations. Given the extraordinary complexity of the human mind and personality the comprehension of behavior, desires, memories, goals and attitudes have to find an explanation in an organ weighting about 1.5 kilograms and composed of about 10,000 millions of individual cells with countless interconnections whose byproduct is a unique individual mind, the world contains 6.5 billion individuals, each one of them with a unique personality and mind. So, although concepts as happiness, fulfillment, love, sadness, and aspirations are easy to define in generic terms each individual expresses these sensations in a different and irreproducible way. Yet, some feelings and desires are common to all human beings, no matter his or her socioeconomic condition nor race, gender, location or cultural status; impressed in the mind of all human beings is the desire for happiness, for pleasure, for plenitude, they are attached to an instinctive aversion to pain, to sadness, to emotional suffering and to depression. Moreover, we as the most sophisticated creatures (thanks to our brain) are endowed with all kind of biological and psychological mechanisms to search instinctively for satisfaction and fear for sadness. Among these mechanisms in the brain exist various pathways, neural areas, cellular receptors, neurotransmitters and peptides devoted, some of them entirely, to the sensations of reward, enjoyment and pleasure. All these cellular and molecular structures are already immersed within the most important areas of the human brain, ready at all times to do their job, to induce pleasant sensations in the brain (therefore in the whole individual); they can be activated by countless means of physical, chemical or psychological nature. The amazing feature is that the mechanisms for reward and recreation inside the brain are strictly of biochemical origin, nonetheless the triggering factors can be physical or psychological or a combination of both. Examples are many, in natural conditions, perhaps the most physical origin of a pleasant sensation in the human brain is the sexual arousal and orgasm, whereas the most psychological could be the achievement of a long waited success, whether material or immaterial. In between these two sources of happiness there are all kind of combinations in the everyday life of most humans which constitute in major or minor grade a potential source of pleasure and bring excitement and variety to the otherwise rather simple life which most other beings in the animal kingdom have; where the most conspicuous source of pleasure is the obtention of food; even sexual encounters as source of pleasure are rather occasional, fast and without tangible and long-lasting pleasurable consequences, other than the accomplishment of reproduction.

Along the history of civilization it seems that the remarkable sites for pleasant sensations in the human brain have been a powerful incentive for the creation of art, culinary sophistication, literature, music and religious experiences. Even the every day, recurrent activities like sport and professional goals are driven, at least in part, by the search of pleasant sensations conducted by the usual functioning of the human brain. Thus, eating, drinking, watching a movie, chatting, reading, or walking are experiences that might arouse feelings of pleasure, even subtle ones. These powerful biological structures are immersed on every one and ready to be triggered even by trivial stimulus, this force works parallel, although subjective, to the aversion to sadness, or at least to boredom.

With this premise in mind it seems easy to understand the source of all addictions: they are acquired by a simple and understandable motif in our continuous search for pleasure, all addictive substances share this common origin. What to do to contain the skyrocketing frequency of addictions all over the world? Is it possible to eliminate them, or at least to diminish them, or at the very least to contain them at current figures? Or, as some forecasts predict, addictions are stronger than human ingenuity.

Humans recur to neurotropic substances to have a fast and predictable sensation of pleasure, most use this track as an essential part of modern society; to smoke a cigarette, to have a drink, to use a psychotropic medicine, to inhale marihuana, or to consume any other recreational substance share this goal. The abuse and repetitious use of any one of them might lead to addiction and to a chain of medical disorders either systemic or neurologic where there is a progressively minor achievement of pleasure together with a growing need for the substance in order to prevent unpleasant sensations; a panorama rather different from the initial pleasant feelings obtained, before the addiction developed. A fundamental question is how to break this continuum that unfolds in a large proportion of subjects who are commonly exposed to recreational substances.

I do not forsee any single strategy upon which we could predict a sensible triumph on the fight against addictions; though it seems logical that a change in the current values of society might influence this widespread phenomenon. Perhaps old concepts as the exercise of temperance and educational programs on the futility of artificial sources of happiness and pleasure could modify the endless pursuit for enjoyment so characteristic of our times, which is bound to a progressively low tolerance to the frustration, boredom and disappointment that frequently accompany our daily life. It could be useful to teach our children that happiness is by no means a permanent state of mind, but a set of occasional events which must be captured and enjoyed as they pass. It is possible that in our fight against addictions we will have to change the essential philosophy that rules modern society.

INDEX

D

E

F

G

H

S

T